Carrying on in Key Stage 1

Providing continuity in purposeful play and exploration

Outdoor Play

Ros Bayley, Lynn Broadbent, Sally Featherstone

Reprinted 2009
Published 2008 by A&C Black Publishers Limited
36 Soho Square, London W1D 3QY
www.acblack.com

ISBN 978-1-906029-12-8

First published 2008 by Featherstone Education Limited

Text © Ros Bayley, Lyn Broadbent, Sally Featherstone 2008
Illustrations © Kerry Ingham 2008
Photographs © Lynn Broadbent, Ros Bayley,
Sally Featherstone, Sarah Featherstone 2008

A CIP record for this publication is available from the British Library.

Printed in Malta by Gutenberg Press Ltd

This book is produced using paper that is made from wood grown in
managed, sustainable forests. It is natural, renewable and recyclable.
The logging and manufacturing processes conform to the environmental
regulations of the country of origin.

To see our full range of titles

visit www.acblack.com

Contents

Carrying on in Key Stage One

This series of books is intended to support the continuing growth and development of independent learning and practical activities, which are key features of the Early Years Foundation Stage.

Children in Key Stage One need and deserve the chance to build on the best of practice in the Early Years Foundation Stage, which carefully balances adult directed tasks with learning that children initiate and develop themselves, often in the company of responsive adults. These activities, which include sand and water play, construction, role play, independent mark making and writing, creative work, dance and movement, and outdoor play, are some of the activities children value most and miss most in Years One and Two.

> Parent: 'What's it like in Year 1?'
>
> Child: 'There en't no sand and the work's too 'ard.'

This quote from a Year 1 boy echoes the feelings of many children who need to continue the learning styles and situations offered in Reception classes. However, many teachers in Key Stage One feel intense pressure to concentrate on activities that require recording and increasing levels of direction by adults. Why is this, and is it right for teachers to feel so pressured?

One thing we know from research is that practical activity and independent learning are essential for brain growth and reinforcement of growing abilities throughout childhood, at least till the onset of puberty, and for many children this is a lifelong need. We also know that the embedding of learning and the transformation of this into real understanding takes time and practice. Skills need to be reinforced by revisiting them in many different contexts in child initiated learning, and practical challenges, and practical tasks in real life situations will be far more effective than rote learning, worksheets or adult direction.

> 'I hear and I forget,
>
> I see and I remember,
>
> I do and I understand.'
>
> Ancient Chinese Proverb

It is also clear from brain research that many boys (and some girls) are just not ready by the end of Reception to embark on a formal curriculum which involves a lot of sitting down, listening and writing. Their bodies and their brains still need action, challenge and freedom to explore materials and resources in freedom.

But this does not mean that challenge should be absent from such activity! The brain feeds on challenge and novelty, so teachers and other adults working in Key Stage One need to structure the experiences, so they build on existing skills and previous activities, while presenting new opportunities to explore familiar materials in new and exciting ways. Such challenges and activities can:

- 🔥 be led by the Programme of Study for Key Stage One;
- 🔥 focus on thinking skills and personal capabilities;
- 🔥 relate to real world situations and stimuli;
- 🔥 help children to achieve the five outcomes for Every Child Matters.

EVERY CHILD MATTERS
The five outcomes:
Enjoy and achieve
Stay safe
Be healthy
Make a positive contribution
Achieve economic well-being

In **Carrying on in Key Stage 1**, we aim to give you the rationale, the process and the confidence to continue a practical, child centred curriculum which also helps you as teachers to recognise the requirements of the **statutory curriculum for Key Stage One**. Each book in the series follows the same format, and addresses objectives from many areas of the National Curriculum. Of course, when children work on practical challenges, curriculum elements become intertwined, and many will be going on simultaneously.

The Role of the Adult

Of course, even during child initiated learning, **the role of the adult is crucial**. Sensitive adults play many roles as they support, challenge and engage the children in their care. High quality teaching is not easy! If teachers want to expand experiences and enhance learning, they need to be able to stand back, to work alongside, _and_ extend or scaffold the children's learning by offering provocations and challenges to their thinking and activity. The diagram below attempts to describe this complex task, and the way that adults move around the elements in the circle of learning. For ease of reading we have described the elements in the following way, and each double page spread covers all three of the vital roles adults play.

Recognising and building on the practical activities which children have experienced before

This element of the process is vital in scaffolding children's learning so it makes sense to them. Your knowledge of the Foundation Stage curriculum and the way it is organised will be vital in knowing where to start. Teachers and other adults should have first hand knowledge of both the resources and the activities which have been available and how they have been offered in both child initiated and adult led activities. This knowledge should be gained by visiting the Reception classes in action, and by talking to adults and children as they work. Looking at Reception planning will also help.

Understanding the range of adult roles, and the effect different roles have on children's learning

Responsive adults react in different ways to what they see and hear during the day. This knowledge will influence the way they plan for further experiences which meet emerging needs and build on individual interests. The diagram illustrates the complex and interlinking ways in which adults interact with children's learning. Observing, co-playing and extending learning often happen simultaneously, flexibly and sometime unconsciously. It is only when we reflect on our work with children that we realise what a complex and skilled activity is going on.

Offering challenges and provocations

As the adults collect information about the learning, they begin to see how they can help children to extend and scaffold their thinking and learning. The adults offer challenges or provocations which act like grit in an oyster, provoking the children to produce responses and think in new ways about what they know and can do.

Linking the learning with the skills and content of the curriculum

As the children grapple with new concepts and skills, adults can make direct links with curriculum intentions and content. These links can be mapped out across the range of knowledge, skills and understanding contained in the curriculum guidance for Key Stage One. It is also possible to map the development of thinking skills, personal capabilities and concepts which link the taught curriculum with the real world.

The adult as extender of learning
discusses ideas
shares thinking
makes new possibilities evident
instigates new opportunities for learning
extends and builds on learning and interests
supports children in making links in learning
models new skills and techniques

The adult as co-player
shares responsibility with the child
offers suggestions
asks open questions
responds sensitively
models and imitates
plays alongside

The adult as observer
listens attentively
observes carefully
records professionally
interprets skilfully

Looking for the Learning

As children plan, explore, invent, extend, construct, discuss, question and predict in the rich experiences planned and offered, they will communicate what they are learning through speech and actions, as well as through the outcomes of activities. Assessment for learning involves adults and children in discussing and analysing what they discover. Reflecting on learning, through discussion with other children and adults, is a key factor in securing skills and abilities, fixing and 'hard wiring' the learning in each child's brain. And, of course, teachers and other adults need to recognise, confirm and record children's achievements, both for the self esteem this brings to the children and to fulfil their own duties as educators.

You could find out what children already know and have experienced by:

* talking to them as individuals and in small groups;

* talking to parents and other adults who know them well (teaching assistants are often wonderful sources of information about individual children);

* visiting the Reception classes and looking at spaces, storage and access to resources, including the use of these out of doors;

* providing free access to materials and equipment and watching how children use them when you are not giving any guidance;

* talking as a group or class about what children already know about the materials and those they particularly enjoy using.

Using the curriculum grid to observe, to recognise learning and celebrate achievement

At the end of each section you will find a curriculum grid which covers the whole Programme of Study for Key Stage 1. This is a 'shorthand version' of the full grid included at the end of the book on pages 69-74. A black and white photocopiable version of the grid appears on page 8, so you can make your own copies for planning and particularly for recording observations.

We suggest that as the children work on the provocations and other challenges in this book, adults (teachers and teaching assistants) can use the grid to observe groups of children and record the areas of the curriculum they are covering in their work. The grids can also be used to record what children say and describe in plenary sessions and other discussions.

These observations will enable you to recognise the learning that happens as children explore the materials and engage with the challenging questions you ask and the problems you pose. And of course, as you observe, you will begin to see what needs to happen next; identifying the next steps in learning! This logical and vital stage in the process may identify:

* some children who will be ready for more of the same activity;

* some who need to repeat and reinforce previous stages;

* some who need to relate skills to new contexts, the same activity or skill practiced in a new place or situation;

* some who will want to extend or sustain the current activity in time, space or detail;

* others who will wish to record their work in photos, drawings, models, stories, video etc.

Critical and Thinking Skills

The grid also identifies the key skills which children need for thinking about and evaluating their work. Many schools now observe and evaluate how well these skills are developing when children work on challenging projects and investigations.

"The natural world is a place for exploration, learning about risk, building confidence and escaping into the imagination."
Fiona Danks & Jo Schofield in 'Nature's Playground'

Going Further

Offering extension activities is a way of scaffolding children's learning, taking the known into the unknown, the familiar into the new, the secure into the challenging. It is the role of the adult to turn their knowledge of the children into worthwhile, long term lines of enquiry and development which will become self-sustaining and last throughout life.

At the end of each section in the book you will find a selection of useful resources, links and other information to help you bring construction to life. You could use these resources by encouraging individuals and groups:

* to **use the Internet** to find images and information;

* to **use ICT equipment** such as cameras, tape recorders, video and dictaphones to record their explorations and experiments;

* to **explore information books** in libraries and other places at home and at school;

* to **make contact by email and letter** with experts, craftsmen, artists, manufacturers, suppliers and other contacts;

* to **make books, films, PowerPoint presentations**;

* to **record their work** in photographs and other media;

* to **respond to stimuli** such as photographs, video, exhibitions and other creative stimuli;

* to **look at the built and natural environment** with curiosity, interest and creativity;

* to **become involved in preserving the natural world**, develop environmental awareness and support recycling;

* to **look at the world of work** and extend their ideas of what they might become and how they might live their lives;

* to **develop a sense of economic awareness** and the world of work in its widest sense;

* to **feel a sense of community** and to explore how they might make a contribution to the school and wider communities in which they live;

* to **work together and develop the ability to think, reason and solve problems** in their learning.

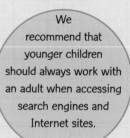

We recommend that younger children should always work with an adult when accessing search engines and Internet sites.

The suggested resources include websites, books, contacts and addresses. There are also some photographs which may inspire young learners as they work on the provocations and challenges suggested.

We hope you will find the ideas in this book useful in stimulating your work with children in Year 1 and Year 2. The ideas, photos and provocations we have included are only a start to your thinking and exploring together, of course you and the children will have many more as you start to expand the work they do in these practical areas, providing a rich curriculum base using familiar and well loved materials.

Ros Bayley, Lynn Broadbent, Sally Featherstone: 2007

Literacy

	Lit 1 speak	Lit 2 listen	Lit 3 group	Lit 4 drama	Lit 5 word	Lit 6 spell	Lit 7 text1	Lit 8 text2	Lit 9 text3	Lit10 text4	Lit11 sentence	Lit12 present-ation
	1.1	2.1	3.1	4.1	5.1	6.1	7.1	8.1	9.1	10.1	11.1	12.1
	1.2	2.2	3.2	4.2	5.2	6.2	7.2	8.2	9.2	10.2	11.2	12.2

Numeracy

	Num 1 U&A	Num 2 count	Num 3 number	Num 4 calculate	Num 5 shape	Num 6 measure	Num 7 data
	1.1	2.1	3.1	4.1	5.1	6.1	7.1
	1.2	2.2	3.2	4.2	5.2	6.2	7.2

Date	
Names	

Science

	SC1 Enquiry			SC2 Life processes					SC3 Materials		SC4 Phys processes		
	Sc1.1	Sc1.2	Sc1.3	Sc2.1	Sc2.2	Sc2.3	Sc2.4	Sc2.5	Sc3.1	Sc3.2	Sc4.1	Sc4.2	Sc4.3
	1.1a	1.2a	1.3a	2.1a	2.2a	2.3a	2.4a	2.5a	3.1a	3.2a	4.1a	4.2a	4.3a
	1.1b	1.2b	1.3b	2.1b	2.2b	2.3b	2.4b	2.5b	3.1b	3.2b	4.1b	4.2b	4.3b
	1.1c	1.2c	1.3c	2.1c	2.2c	2.3c		2.5c	3.1c		4.1c	4.2c	4.3c
	1.1d				2.2d				3.1d				4.3d
					2.2e								
					2.2f								
					2.2g								

ICT

	ICT 1 finding out		ICT 2 ideas	ICT 3 reviewing	ICT 4 breadth
	1.1a	1.2a	2a	3a	4a
	1.1b	1.2b	2b	3b	4b
	1.1c	`1.2c	2c	3c	4c
		1.2d			

History

	H1 chronology	H2 events, people	H3 interpret	H4 enquire	H5 org & comm	H6 breadth
	1a	2a	3a	4a	5a	6a
	1b	2b		4b		6b
						6c
						6d

Geography

	G1.1 & G1.2 enquiry		G2 places	G3 processes	G4 environment	G5 breadth
	1.1a	1.2a	2a	3a	4a	5a
	1.1b	1.2b	2b	3b	4b	5b
	1.1c	1.2c	2c			5c
	1.1d	1.2d	2d			5d
			2e			

PE

	PE1 devel skills	PE2 apply skills	PE3 evaluate	PE4 fitness	PE5 breadth
	1a	2a	3a	4a	5a dance
	1b	2b	3b	4b	5b games
		2c	3c		5c gym

Art & Design

	A&D1 ideas	A&D2 making	A&D3 evaluating	A&D4 materials	A&D5 breadth
	1a	2a	3a	4a	5a
	1b	2b	3b	4b	5b
		2c		4c	5c
					5d

PHSE & C

	PSHEC1 conf & resp	PSHEC2 citizenship	PSHEC3 health	PSHEC4 relationships
	1a	2a	3a	4a
	1b	2b	3b	4b
	1c	2c	3c	4c
	1d	2d	3d	4d
	1e	2e	3e	4e
		2f	3f	
		2g	3g	
		2h		

D&T

	D&T 1 developing	D&T 2 tool use	D&T 3 evaluating	D&T 4 materials	D&T 5 breadth
	1a	2a	3a	4a	5a
	1b	2b	3b	4b	5b
	1c	2c			5c
	1d	2d			
	1e	2e			

Music

	M1 performing	M2 composing	M3 appraising	M4 listening	M5 breadth
	1a	2a	3a	4a	5a
	1b	2b	3b	4b	5b
	1c			4c	5c
					5d

Key to KS1 PoS on Pages 69-74

Critical Skills	Thinking Skills
problem solving	observing
decision making	classifying
critical thinking	prediction
creative thinking	making inferences
communication	problem solving
organisation	drawing conclusions
management	
leadership	

Notes on how to take the learning forward:

Tyres, Ropes and Pulleys

Tyres, Ropes and Pulleys

Previous experience in the Foundation Stage.
Most children will have had experience of using these sorts of resources, and some will have had free access to them for building their own structures and experimenting with these materials in:

* free play, constructing, lifting, tying, pulling;
* rolling tyres, building towers;
* tying pulleys and ropes to climbing frames and other fixed apparatus;
* lifting buckets and baskets, full or empty;
* attaching to wheeled vehicles for pulling and fixing;
* games involving jumping on, in and over tyres and ropes;
* making shelters and dens with ropes, fabrics and other construction materials.

Pause for thought

In the early stages of working with these materials it is crucial to continue to observe the children. Only by doing this can you set developmentally appropriate challenges and provocations. The ideas listed here are offered as suggestions; the most exciting challenges will arise from children's own interests and motivations, which will only become apparent as you spend time with them, watching and joining them in their play. As you do this, you will be moving between the three interconnecting roles of observer, co-player, extender described below, and will be able to decide what you need to do next to take the learning forward.

The responsive adult (see page 5)

In three interconnecting roles, the responsive adult will be:

observer
* observing
* listening
* interpreting

co-player
* modelling
* playing alongside
* offering suggestions
* responding sensitively
* initiating with care!

extender
* discussing ideas
* sharing thinking
* modelling new skills
* asking open questions
* being an informed extender
* instigating ideas & thoughts
* supporting children as they make links in learning
* making possibilities evident
* introducing new ideas and resources
* offering challenges and provocations

Offering Challenges and Provocations - some ideas:

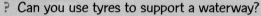

As children get older they can use ropes, pulleys and tyres in conjunction with other flexible resources to experiment with materials, structures and forces. They may need some support at the start, if these resources are not familiar to them, but once they are used to flexible materials they will be able to respond to all sorts of scientific and technological challenges.

? Can you use tyres to support a waterway?

? How can you use a pulley to lift a basket higher than your head? How can you fix the rope so the basket stays up?

? Look at some pictures of flagpoles, or a real one if you know where to find one. How do flagpoles work and how does the flag go up and down on the rope?

? Use a piece of fabric to make a flag. Paint a design on it and find a place where you could fly the flag. Use thin rope to make a pulley, so you can raise and lower your flag when you need to.

? Make some bunting for your outdoor area. Bunting is lots of little flags in a row. Hang it on a rope with a pulley.

? Look at some tyres on Google. How many different sorts can you find? Now find some tyres in the Lego or toy car tyres. How do tyres work? What are they made from?

? Use the toy tyres to make a painting by rolling them in paint and then using them to print on paper.

? Now try spreading some paint or mud on a flat surface outside and using the tyres to make tracks. Photograph the different tracks. Try the same thing with some real tyres.

? Use the tyres in your outdoor area to build a tower - how high can you build it? Can you make the tyres into a tunnel?

? Make up a game with tyres and ropes, where you have to jump, go through, over and under. Use chalk to make markings if you need them. Then invite your friends to play the game and see who is best at it.

Ready for more?

- Find out about prayer flags by putting 'prayer flags' in Google images. Can you make some prayer flags for your outdoor area? - decorate them with pictures, patterns or words.

- Find some pulleys and rope. Can you make a pulley system that will lift a weight that you can't easily lift yourself? Putting the heavy things in a bucket or container with a handle will help. Take some photos of your experiments.

- Find a colander or sieve, and find a way to suspend it above a bucket or water tray (look at the pictures here). Can you raise and lower the colander by using a simple pulley?

- If you can get a bike to look at, investigate how the cogs in bike chains work. Draw a diagram of the chain and cogs of a bike and label all the parts. Now describe how it works.

- Find out about the sorts of pulleys used by sailors, firemen, farmers, vets, Air Sea Rescue helicopters. You can look in books or on the internet. Make a book of your findings.

- Use tyres to make these things:
  - a flower planter
  - a sand pit
  - a pond that holds water
  - a bog garden.

  Take photos of your inventions.

Materials, equipment, suppliers, websites, books and other references

For simple pulleys, use:
* cotton reels or bobbins to wind string or rope round;
* short lengths of hard plastic tubing;
* pieces from construction sets such as Lego, Gears or Connect
* the hubs from toy cars, with the tyres removed

For pulleys with ropes try:
www.tts-group.co.uk www.mindstretchers or www.ascoeducational.co.uk or www.eduzone.co.uk

Contact any tyre fitting business and they will probably be delighted to give you some tyres. They may even deliver them to you! Some tyres leave a black residue on hands and clothing, so check the ones you use.

Google 'tyre' 'pulley' 'flagpole'

Some **websites**:

www.ise5-14.org.uk/Prim3/New_guidelines/Newsletters (newsletter & challenges)
automata.co.uk/pulleys - for moving figures
www.ehow.com/how_1277_make-simple-pulley - activity
www.mikids.com/Smachines - pulleys
www.sciencetech.technomuses.ca/english/schoolzone/activities (pulley activity sheet)
www.42explore.com/smplmac - links to lots of websites for simple mechanics
outreach.rice.edu - teacher materials
www.dorsetforyou.com/media/pdf/r/b/Pre_school_outdoor_environment.pdf - for a downloadable booklet on outdoor play with a section on tyres
www.ehow.com/how_1276_build-block-tackle
www.athropolis.com/links/how-work - how lots of things work

Some suitable **books** for younger readers include:

Pulleys (Simple Machines); Michael Dahl; Franklin Watts Ltd
Levers (Simple Machines); Michael Dahl; Franklin Watts Ltd
Levers Big Book (Very Useful Machines); Chris Oxlade; Heinemann
Pulleys (Very Useful Machines); Chris Oxlade; Heinemann Library
Ramps and Wedges (Very Useful Machines); Chris Oxlade; Heinemann Library
Amazing Machines (Design Challenge); Keith Good; Evans Brothers Ltd
Play Equipment for Kids; Great Projects You Can Build; Storey Books, US

Curriculum coverage grid overleaf

Potential NC KS1 Curriculum Coverage through the provocations suggested for tyres, ropes and pulleys.

Literacy

	Lit 1 speak	Lit 2 listen	Lit 3 group	Lit 4 drama	Lit 5 word	Lit 6 spell	Lit 7 text1	Lit 8 text2	Lit 9 text3	Lit10 text4	Lit11 sentence	Lit12 presentation
	1.1	2.1	3.1	4.1	5.1	6.1	7.1	8.1	9.1	10.1	11.1	12.1
	1.2	2.2	3.2	4.2	5.2	6.2	7.2	8.2	9.2	10.2	11.2	12.2

Numeracy

	Num 1 U&A	Num 2 count	Num 3 number	Num 4 calculate	Num 5 shape	Num 6 measure	Num 7 data
	1.1	2.1	3.1	4.1	5.1	6.1	7.1
	1.2	2.2	3.2	4.2	5.2	6.2	7.2

Science

	SC1 Enquiry			SC2 Life processes					SC3 Materials		SC4 Phys processes		
	Sc1.1	Sc1.2	Sc1.3	Sc2.1	Sc2.2	Sc2.3	Sc2.4	Sc2.5	Sc3.1	Sc3.2	Sc4.1	Sc4.2	Sc4.3
	1.1a	1.2a	1.3a	2.1a	2.2a	2.3a	2.4a	2.5a	3.1a	3.2a	4.1a	4.2a	4.3a
	1.1b	1.2b	1.3b	2.1b	2.2b	2.3b	2.4b	2.5b	3.1b	3.2b	4.1b	4.2b	4.3b
	1.1c	1.2c	1.3c	2.1c	2.2c	2.3c		2.5c	3.1c		4.1c	4.2c	4.3c
	1.1d				2.2d				3.1d				4.3d
					2.2e								
					2.2f								
					2.2g								

ICT

	ICT 1 finding out		ICT 2 ideas	ICT 3 reviewing	ICT 4 breadth
	1.1a	1.2a	2a	3a	4a
	1.1b	1.2b	2b	3b	4b
	1.1c	1.2c	2c	3c	4c
		1.2d			

Full version of KS1 PoS on pages 69-74
Photocopiable version on page 8

D&T

	D&T 1 developing	D&T 2 tool use	D&T 3 evaluating	D&T 4 materials	D&T 5 breadth
	1a	2a	3a	4a	5a
	1b	2b	3b	4b	5b
	1c	2c			5c
	1d	2d			
	1e	2e			

History

	H1 chronology	H2 events, people	H3 interpret	H4 enquire	H5 org & comm	H6 breadth
	1a	2a	3a	4a	5a	6a
	1b	2b		4b		6b
						6c
						6d

Geography

	G1.1 & G1.2 enquiry		G2 places	G3 processes	G4 environment	G5 breadth
	1.1a	1.2a	2a	3a	4a	5a
	1.1b	1.2b	2b	3b	4b	5b
	1.1c	1.2c	2c			5c
	1.1d	1.2d	2d			5d
			2e			

Music

	M1 performing	M2 composing	M3 appraising	M4 listening	M5 breadth
	1a	2a	3a	4a	5a
	1b	2b	3b	4b	5b
	1c			4c	5c
					5d

PHSE & C

	PSHEC1 conf & resp	PSHEC2 citizenship	PSHEC3 health	PSHEC4 relationships
	1a	2a	3a	4a
	1b	2b	3b	4b
	1c	2c	3c	4c
	1d	2d	3d	4d
	1e	2e	3e	4e
		2f	3f	
		2g	3g	
		2h		

Art & Design

	A&D1 ideas	A&D2 making	A&D3 evaluating	A&D4 materials	A&D5 breadth
	1a	2a	3a	4a	5a
	1b	2b	3b	4b	5b
		2c		4c	5c
					5d

PE

	PE1 devel skills	PE2 apply skills	PE3 evaluate	PE4 fitness	PE5 breadth
	1a	2a	3a	4a	5a dance
	1b	2b	3b	4b	5b games
		2c	3c		5c gym

Critical skills	Thinking Skills
problem solving	observing
decision making	classifying
critical thinking	prediction
creative thinking	making inferences
communication	problem solving
organisation	drawing conclusions
management	
leadership	

Boxes and Cartons

Boxes and Cartons

Previous experience in the Foundation Stage.

Empty cardboard boxes are a free resource for all schools are now a feature of most early years settings, and the majority of children will have experimented with and explored these resources in:

* building and stacking;
* assembling and dis-assembling;
* to make homes and habitats for
  toys
  vehicles
  puppets;
* building small worlds;
* making dens;
* cutting boxes up to make other things;
* fitting boxes inside each other;
* making parcels and presents.

Pause for thought

In the early stages of working with these materials it is crucial to continue to observe the children. Only by doing this can you set developmentally appropriate challenges and provocations. The ideas listed here are offered as suggestions; the most exciting challenges will arise from children's own interests and motivations, which will only become apparent as you spend time with them, watching and joining them in their play. As you do this, you will be moving between the three interconnecting roles of observer, co-player, extender described below, and will be able to decide what you need to do next to take the learning forward.

The responsive adult (see page 5)

In three interconnecting roles, the responsive adult will be:

observer

* observing
* listening
* interpreting

co-player

* modelling
* playing alongside
* offering suggestions
* responding sensitively
* initiating with care!

extender

* discussing ideas
* sharing thinking
* modelling new skills
* asking open questions
* being an informed extender
* instigating ideas & thoughts
* supporting children as they make links in learning
* making possibilities evident
* introducing new ideas and resources
* offering challenges and provocations

Offering Challenges and Provocations - some ideas:

? Can you use boxes to create:
  a home for a soft toy
  a garage for a car or truck
  a home for a small world character?
? Can you join cardboard boxes together to make a tunnel? Is it big enough for you to crawl through?
? What is the longest tunnel you can make?
? Can you create a tunnel that goes round corners?
? Can you fix cartons or boxes together to make a tower taller than you? Now find three different ways to measure your tower.
? Can you use boxes and cartons to make:
  a suit of armour?
  a hobby horse?
  a space-suit?
  a robot?
  a windmill?
  a Chinese dragon?
? Find some corrugated cardboard. How can you use this to make printed patterns?
? Can you make a notice board from the card from boxes? Make your notice board attractive, and find a way to hang it up, indoors or outside.
? Can you use big cardboard boxes to make a den for yourself and your friends? Put 'building dens' into Google to get some ideas.
? Cut a very big box up to make a puppet theatre, find some puppets and then make up a puppet show for your friends.
? Make a TV set that you can put over your head. Now can you be a weather presenter or a comedian?
? What can you use to waterproof a cardboard box. Try some of your ideas.

Ready for more?

☚ Can you use boxes to make a den with more than one room? Then can you make your den fold up so you can store it?

☚ Can you find a way to paint or wallpaper the inside of your den? What is the best material to use?

☚ Google 'cardboard classroom' or 'westborough school' to find a school classroom that really is made from cardboard. How do you think they made it?

☚ Can you make some windows and a door in your house?

☚ Put 'cardboard furniture' in Google and find some designs and ideas for making your own. Then put www.paperpod.co.uk in a search and see what you can find. You could send for a catalogue or try to make a cardboard chair or rocket yourselves.

☚ Cut some shapes from the cardboard and add things to them to make a mobile for your classroom. Can you make it waterproof so it can hang outside? Can you make a musical mobile by adding things to the cardboard?

☚ Find some strong boxes and make a drum kit. What will you use for drumsticks?

☚ Can you turn a box into a weaving loom? What do you need to add? Does it work?

☚ Can you use the cardboard from a carton to make a small gift box or a habitat for a small creature?

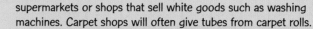

Materials, equipment, suppliers, websites, books and other references

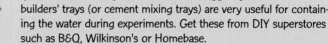

You can get boxes, cartons and tyres from:

- supermarkets or shops that sell white goods such as washing machines. Carpet shops will often give tubes from carpet rolls.
- tyre service centres such as Kwik-Fit will be glad to get rid of tyres, and some may have tractor and digger tyres too.
- builders' trays (or cement mixing trays) are very useful for containing the water during experiments. Get these from DIY superstores such as B&Q, Wilkinson's or Homebase.
- bargain or 'Pound' shops are good sources for plastic crates, boxes and bowls of all sizes and shapes.
- supermarkets and diaries will specialise in vegetable, drink and milk bottle crates.

Google Images 'cardboard box' 'chair cardboard box' 'rocket cardboard box' 'cardboard box house/castle'.

www.make-stuff.com/kids - has some great projects including a cardboard castle.

www.terragenesis.co.uk - model castle using textured paint.

www.360models.co.uk - is an architectural model site - look at their gallery of models for ideas.

www.ecocentric.co.uk - sell a model castle and other toys made from recycled cardboard.

Some suitable **books** for younger readers include:

Fiction
- My Cat Likes to Hide in Boxes; Eve Sutton; Puffin Books
- Not a Box; Antoinette Portis; HarperCollins Children's Books
- The Shoe Box; Francine Rivers; Tyndale House Publishers
- Jack in a Box; Julia Jarman; HarperCollins Children's Books

Non Fiction
- The Little Book of Bricks and Boxes; Clare Beswick; Featherstone Education
- Creative Crafts from Cardboard Boxes; Nikki Conner; Copper Beech Books
- The Cardboard Box Book; Watson-Guptill Publications
- Milk Carton Mania; Christine M. Irvin; Children's Press
- Egg Carton Mania; Christine M. Irvin; Children's Press
- Likable Recyclables; Linda Schwartz; Learning Works
- Look What You Can Make with Boxes; Lorianne Siomades; Boyds Mills Press
- (also: Look What you can Make With Tubes; Egg Cartons; Craft Sticks; Plastic Bottles; Paper Bags; Newspapers Magazines and Greeting Cards; Plastic Trays; Paper Plates)
- Make It with Cardboard; Anna Olimos Plomer; Book House
- The Big Box; Toni Morrison; Saint Martin's Press Inc.
- The Big Brown Box; Marisabina Russo; HarperCollins
- The Big, Beautiful, Brown Box; Larry Dane Brimner; Children's Press

Curriculum coverage grid overleaf

Potential NC KS1 Curriculum Coverage through the provocations suggested for boxes and cartons.

Full version of KS1 PoS on pages 69-74
Photocopiable version on page 8

Literacy

	Lit 1 speak	Lit 2 listen	Lit 3 group	Lit 4 drama	Lit 5 word	Lit 6 spell	Lit 7 text1	Lit 8 text2	Lit 9 text3	Lit10 text4	Lit11 sentence	Lit12 presentation
Literacy	1.1	2.1	3.1	4.1	5.1	6.1	7.1	8.1	9.1	10.1	11.1	12.1
	1.2	2.2	3.2	4.2	5.2	6.2	7.2	8.2	9.2	10.2	11.2	12.2

Numeracy

	Num 1 U&A	Num 2 count	Num 3 number	Num 4 calculate	Num 5 shape	Num 6 measure	Num 7 data
Numeracy	1.1	2.1	3.1	4.1	5.1	6.1	7.1
	1.2	2.2	3.2	4.2	5.2	6.2	7.2

Science

	SC1 Enquiry			SC2 Life processes					SC3 Materials		SC4 Phys processes		
	Sc1.1	Sc1.2	Sc1.3	Sc2.1	Sc2.2	Sc2.3	Sc2.4	Sc2.5	Sc3.1	Sc3.2	Sc4.1	Sc4.2	Sc4.3
	1.1a	1.2a	1.3a	2.1a	2.2a	2.3a	2.4a	2.5a	3.1a	3.2a	4.1a	4.2a	4.3a
	1.1b	1.2b	1.3b	2.1b	2.2b	2.3b	2.4b	2.5b	3.1b	3.2b	4.1b	4.2b	4.3b
Science	1.1c	1.2c	1.3c	2.1c	2.2c	2.3c		2.5c	3.1c		4.1c	4.2c	4.3c
	1.1d				2.2d				3.1d				4.3d
					2.2e								
					2.2f								
					2.2g								

ICT

	ICT 1 finding out		ICT 2 ideas	ICT 3 reviewing	ICT 4 breadth
	1.1a	1.2a	2a	3a	4a
ICT	1.1b	1.2b	2b	3b	4b
	1.1c	1.2c	2c	3c	4c
		1.2d			

D&T

	D&T 1 developing	D&T 2 tool use	D&T 3 evaluating	D&T 4 materials	D&T 5 breadth
	1a	2a	3a	4a	5a
	1b	2b	3b	4b	5b
D&T	1c	2c			5c
	1d	2d			
	1e	2e			

History

	H1 chronology	H2 events, people	H3 interpret	H4 enquire	H5 org & comm	H6 breadth
	1a	2a	3a	4a	5a	6a
History	1b	2b		4b		6b
						6c
						6d

Geography

	G1.1 & G1.2 enquiry		G2 places	G3 processes	G4 environment	G5 breadth
	1.1a	1.2a	2a	3a	4a	5a
Geography	1.1b	1.2b	2b	3b	4b	5b
	1.1c	1.2c	2c			5c
	1.1d	1.2d	2d			5d
			2e			

Music

	M1 performing	M2 composing	M3 appraising	M4 listening	M5 breadth
	1a	2a	3a	4a	5a
	1b	2b	3b	4b	5b
Music	1c			4c	5c
					5d

PHSE & C

	PSHEC1 conf & resp	PSHEC2 citizenship	PSHEC3 health	PSHEC4 relationships
	1a	2a	3a	4a
	1b	2b	3b	4b
PHSE & C	1c	2c	3c	4c
	1d	2d	3d	4d
	1e	2e	3e	4e
		2f	3f	
		2g	3g	
		2h		

Art & Design

	A&D1 ideas	A&D2 making	A&D3 evaluating	A&D4 materials	A&D5 breadth
	1a	2a	3a	4a	5a
Art& Design	1b	2b	3b	4b	5b
		2c		4c	5c
					5d

PE

	PE1 devel skills	PE2 apply skills	PE3 evaluate	PE4 fitness	PE5 breadth
	1a	2a	3a	4a	5a dance
PE	1b	2b	3b	4b	5b games
		2c	3c		5c gym

Critical skills	Thinking Skills
problem solving	observing
decision making	classifying
critical thinking	prediction
creative thinking	making inferences
communication	problem solving
organisation	drawing conclusions
management	
leadership	

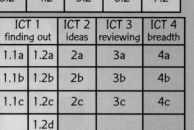

Bricks and Blocks

Bricks and blocks

Previous experience in the Foundation Stage.

By the time children leave the Foundation Stage they should have had wide experience of using bricks and blocks of all sorts and sizes:

* in free play indoors and out of doors;
* to make structures and buildings;
* in play with small world animals and figures;
* to explore balance, stability and form;
* for towers and fantasy landscapes;
* to make child-sized walls, shelters and dens.

They should also have had experience of:

* working on specific projects with bricks, such as making houses for story characters or habitats for creatures;
* experimenting with non-standard units such as sawn logs; and with real bricks.

Pause for thought

In the early stages of working with these materials it is crucial to continue to observe the children. Only by doing this can you set developmentally appropriate challenges and provocations. The ideas listed here are offered as suggestions; the most exciting challenges will arise from children's own interests and motivations, which will only become apparent as you spend time with them, watching and joining them in their play. As you do this, you will be moving between the three interconnecting roles of observer, co-player, extender described below, and will be able to decide what you need to do next to take the learning forward.

The responsive adult (see page 5)

In three interconnecting roles, the responsive adult will be:

* observing
* listening
* interpreting

observer

* modelling
* playing alongside
* offering suggestions
* responding sensitively
* initiating with care!

co-player

* discussing ideas
* sharing thinking
* modelling new skills
* asking open questions
* being an informed extender
* instigating ideas & thoughts
* supporting children as they make links in learning
* making possibilities evident
* introducing new ideas and resources
* offering challenges and provocations

extender

Offering Challenges and Provocations - some ideas:

It is important to find out the breadth of experience children have had during the Early Years Foundation Stage, particularly in using bricks out of doors. You may also want to explore non-standard and real brick units with them exploring the challenges of working with these, before embarking on independent challenges and provocations.

? Get a set of wooden bricks. How many different ways can you sort them before using them to build with? make a chart or take photos to show what you did.

? Can you build a habitat for minibeasts out of doors with bricks or sawn branches? Leave the habitat out for several days and see if any minibeasts move in.

? Try making several different habitats in different places outside. You could add bark, twigs, leaves and other natural materials to the bricks. Take photos of all the habitats and see what happens to them over time.

? Can you make an enclosed structure with wooden bricks? What can you use for a roof?

? Use bricks and guttering to make a water-way or sand-way that goes at least two metres. What is the best way of using the bricks?

? Use real bricks with planks to make a roadway for toy cars. What is the longest roadway you can make. Can you make it in a way that cars will run all the way along it without needing you to push them?

? Can you prop up a drainpipe or cardboard tube with bricks so cars can race down it? Mark where the cars finish and experiment with making a run that propels cars the furthest. Record your results.

? Can you make a structure with bricks that is big enough to get inside?

Ready for more?

- Go outside and look at some walls. Record what you see with a camera. How are brick walls built so they don't fall down? Experiment with making walls with wooden bricks that look like real brick walls.

- Now try this experiment with real bricks. You might be able to use some real cement to fix them together.

- Find some bricks and planks, and experiment with making bridges. What is the longest bridge you can make? How can you prop up the spans? Take photos of your experiments.

- Look at bridges on the internet. What is the longest bridge in the world? Download some pictures from Google or internet sites and use these with your bridge photos to make a book or display. If you laminate the pictures, you could make an outdoor book or display.

- Work with some friends. Use all the bricks and blocks you can find to make a huge construction out of doors. Take as long as you need. Your construction could be a city, a space port, a castle, an airport or any other construction. You could work big, high or wide. Take some photos as you work. Add small world people, animals and vehicles. Make signs and notices. Use chalk or paint if you need it. Invent a name for your construction.

Materials, equipment, suppliers, websites, books and other references

Educational suppliers all have a range of wooden and plastic bricks of various sizes - try www.tts-group.co.uk www.ascoeducational.co.uk or **your local consortium group**.

The best wooden bricks are from Community Playthings www.communityplaythings.co.uk - they are expensive but very hardwearing, precision cut and great to build with. Download a free leaflet on brick building from this site too.

Make your own sets of building blocks from sawn branches (look for some after a storm and saw them into suitable lengths (the children could do this!). Or contact your local Parks Department to see if they can help. They may be able to give you some slices of tree trunks, which give children a real challenge.

Look on **Google Images** 'bricks' 'brick building' 'wooden bricks' 'brick castle' 'children building'. www.diydoctor.org.uk/projects/laybricksandblocks has a sheet on block building with real bricks. www.buildingcentre.co.uk is the centre for the building industry.

Local colleges may have bricklaying courses and students may be able to visit you, and of course, you could ask parents and relatives to come and demonstrate their skills.

Some suitable **books** for younger readers include:

A Day with a Brick Layer; Mark Thomas; Children's Press
Building Tools; Inez Snyder; Children's Press
Building Bridges; David Glover; Longman
Castles; A 3-Dimensional Exploration; Gillian Osband; Tango Books
What Were Castles For?; Phil Roxbee Cox; Usborne Publishing Ltd
A Picture History of Great Buildings; Gillian Clements; Frances Lincoln
The Tallest Buildings; Susan K. Mitchell; Gareth Stevens Publishing
Bridge Building; Diana Briscoe; Red Brick Learning
A City Through Time; Philip Steele; DK Publishing
Atlantis: The Legend of a Lost City; Christina Balit; Frances Lincoln
Ant Cities; Arthur Dorros; Tandem Library
Habitats; Where Wildlife Lives; Sally Hewitt; Franklin Watts Ltd
All Kinds of Habitats; Sally Hewitt; Franklin Watts Ltd
Woodlands; (Wild Habitats of the British Isles); Louise Spilsbury; Heinemann Library
The Great Outdoors; Saving Habitats (You Can Save the Planet); Richard Spilsbury; Heinemann
The Little Book of Garden Wildlife; Laura Howell; Usborne Publishing Ltd
Urban Wildlife; Usborne Publishing Ltd
Local Wildlife; What's in My Garden?; Sally Hewitt; Stargazer Books

Curriculum coverage grid overleaf

Potential NC KS1 Curriculum Coverage through the provocations suggested for bricks and blocks.

Full version of KS1 PoS on pages 69-74
Photocopiable version on page 8

Literacy

Lit 1 speak	Lit 2 listen	Lit 3 group	Lit 4 drama	Lit 5 word	Lit 6 spell	Lit 7 text1	Lit 8 text2	Lit 9 text3	Lit10 text4	Lit11 sentence	Lit12 presentation
1.1	2.1	3.1	4.1	5.1	6.1	7.1	8.1	9.1	10.1	11.1	12.1
1.2	2.2	3.2	4.2	5.2	6.2	7.2	8.2	9.2	10.2	11.2	12.2

Numeracy

Num 1 U&A	Num 2 count	Num 3 number	Num 4 calculate	Num 5 shape	Num 6 measure	Num 7 data
1.1	2.1	3.1	4.1	5.1	6.1	7.1
1.2	2.2	3.2	4.2	5.2	6.2	7.2

Science

SC1 Enquiry			SC2 Life processes					SC3 Materials		SC4 Phys processes		
Sc1.1	Sc1.2	Sc1.3	Sc2.1	Sc2.2	Sc2.3	Sc2.4	Sc2.5	Sc3.1	Sc3.2	Sc4.1	Sc4.2	Sc4.3
1.1a	1.2a	1.3a	2.1a	2.2a	2.3a	2.4a	2.5a	3.1a	3.2a	4.1a	4.2a	4.3a
1.1b	1.2b	1.3b	2.1b	2.2b	2.3b	2.4b	2.5b	3.1b	3.2b	4.1b	4.2b	4.3b
1.1c	1.2c	1.3c	2.1c	2.2c	2.3c		2.5c	3.1c		4.1c	4.2c	4.3c
1.1d				2.2d				3.1d				4.3d
				2.2e								
				2.2f								
				2.2g								

ICT

ICT 1 finding out		ICT 2 ideas	ICT 3 reviewing	ICT 4 breadth
1.1a	1.2a	2a	3a	4a
1.1b	1.2b	2b	3b	4b
1.1c	1.2c	2c	3c	4c
	1.2d			

D&T

D&T 1 developing	D&T 2 tool use	D&T 3 evaluating	D&T 4 materials	D&T 5 breadth
1a	2a	3a	4a	5a
1b	2b	3b	4b	5b
1c	2c			5c
1d	2d			
1e	2e			

History

H1 chronology	H2 events, people	H3 interpret	H4 enquire	H5 org & comm	H6 breadth
1a	2a	3a	4a	5a	6a
1b	2b		4b		6b
					6c
					6d

Geography

G1.1 & G1.2 enquiry		G2 places	G3 processes	G4 environment	G5 breadth
1.1a	1.2a	2a	3a	4a	5a
1.1b	1.2b	2b	3b	4b	5b
1.1c	1.2c	2c			5c
1.1d	1.2d	2d			5d
		2e			

Music

M1 performing	M2 composing	M3 appraising	M4 listening	M5 breadth
1a	2a	3a	4a	5a
1b	2b	3b	4b	5b
1c			4c	5c
				5d

PHSE & C

PSHEC1 conf & resp	PSHEC2 citizenship	PSHEC3 health	PSHEC4 relationships
1a	2a	3a	4a
1b	2b	3b	4b
1c	2c	3c	4c
1d	2d	3d	4d
1e	2e	3e	4e
	2f	3f	
	2g	3g	
	2h		

Art & Design

A&D1 ideas	A&D2 making	A&D3 evaluating	A&D4 materials	A&D5 breadth
1a	2a	3a	4a	5a
1b	2b	3b	4b	5b
	2c		4c	5c
				5d

PE

PE1 devel skills	PE2 apply skills	PE3 evaluate	PE4 fitness	PE5 breadth
1a	2a	3a	4a	5a dance
1b	2b	3b	4b	5b games
	2c	3c		5c gym

Critical skills	Thinking Skills
problem solving	observing
decision making	classifying
critical thinking	prediction
creative thinking	making inferences
communication	problem solving
organisation	drawing conclusions
management	
leadership	

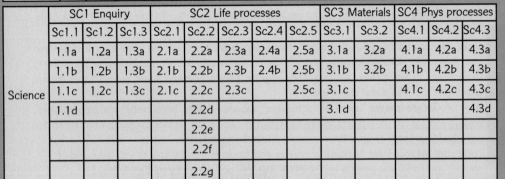

Sound and Music

Sound and Music

Previous experience in the Foundation Stage.
During their time in the Early Years Foundation Stage, children will have explored both home made and commercially produced instruments in a wide range of contexts:

*   in free play indoors and out of doors.

and to:

*   explore and discriminate between sounds;
*   accompany songs and jingles;
*   play listening games;
*   produce sound effects to accompany traditional tales and stories, and to make sound pictures;
*   make music for dances;
*   play along with recorded music.

They should also have listened to a wide range of music from a variety of cultures.

Pause for thought

In the early stages of working with these materials it is crucial to continue to observe the children. Only by doing this can you set developmentally appropriate challenges and provocations. The ideas listed here are offered as suggestions; the most exciting challenges will arise from children's own interests and motivations, which will only become apparent as you spend time with them, watching and joining them in their play. As you do this, you will be moving between the three interconnecting roles of observer, co-player, extender described below, and will be able to decide what you need to do next to take the learning forward.

The responsive adult (see page 5)

In three interconnecting roles, the responsive adult will be:

*   observing
*   listening
*   interpreting

observer

*   modelling
*   playing alongside
*   offering suggestions
*   responding sensitively
*   initiating with care!

co-player

*   discussing ideas
*   sharing thinking
*   modelling new skills
*   asking open questions
*   being an informed extender
*   instigating ideas & thoughts
*   supporting children as they make links in learning
*   making possibilities evident
*   introducing new ideas and resources
*   offering challenges and provocations

extender

Offering Challenges and Provocations - some ideas:

When setting up a music area, try to make it near a dressing up/performance area so these elements of play can be incorporated. A simple CD player is another piece of equipment worth considering.

? Can you design and make an outside music area using found and recycled materials? Look on the Internet for Bash the Trash for ideas. (Other ideas opposite).

? How many different kinds of shakers can you make, using:
    *   paper or plastic cups
    *   tins with lids
    *   bowls and buckets
    *   plastic bottles
    *   bottle tops

and filling them with all sorts of small objects. Which works best? Which makes the best sound? Which is loudest, which is softest?

? Use your shakers to accompany music on a CD or some songs. Can you keep a beat with your shaker?

? Can you make some music with these things:
    *   saucepans?
    *   saucepan lids?
    *   old cutlery?
    *   chains?
    *   plastic bottles?
    *   bottle tops or ring pulls?

? Design and make some instruments for a marching band. Plan your route. Practice some good rhythms that are easy to march to. Have a parade.

? Find some drumsticks or chopsticks, and use these to explore the sounds you can make outside. Which things make the highest sounds, which make the lowest sounds? Can you play a tune?

Ready for more?

- Create sound stories on these themes:
  - a walk in the woods
  - a stormy day
  - a walk on the beach
  - a visit to the zoo
  - a volcano erupting
  - superheroes rescuing someone.
- Choose some of your favourite story books and make up sound effects to accompany the story.
- Make your own drum kit or percussion set from recycled materials.
- Can you use musical instruments to send messages? Work with friends to make a secret message system.
- Research on the internet and in books to find out everything you can about:
  - carnivals
  - circuses
  - festivals
  - talent shows.
- Plan your own show or event.
- Make up some sound games, by recording sounds out of doors and seeing if your friends can guess what they are. Try the games with the children in reception or the nursery.
- Write and perform a sound track for a puppet show or a play you have made up with friends.
- Find some ways of writing down your music, so other people can play it too.

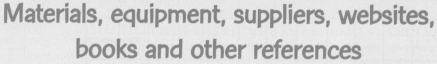

Materials, equipment, suppliers, websites, books and other references

Musical instruments are much more fun out of doors, because the sounds carry further and there is not a limit on noise! You can provide a simple trolley with instruments, fabrics, ribbon sticks and other movement equipment for free expression of specific tasks and challenges. Encourage children to make their own sound makers and instruments as well from recycled and simple materials. The following sites give guidance on providing more permanent musical experiences out of doors, as well as tips on providing simple, inexpensive features to extend creativity through music and dance:

Some **web sites**:

www.bingbangbong.info - for musical instruments
www.mindstretchers.co.uk - more instruments to use out of doors
www.butlersheetmetal.com - make your own steel drum
www.mudcat.org/kids/drums - for simple home-made drums
www.artistshelpingchildren.org - has a page on making your own musical instruments
www.4to40.com - has instructions for a mini-dustbin drum
www.worcestershire.gov.uk - where you can download a free leaflet on outdoor music
www.freenotes.net - an American firm that installs outdoor musical equipment - good picture gallery
www.education-show.com - has information about outdoor music suppliers

Some **book** titles:
101 Music Games for Children; G. Storms; Hunter House
Game-songs with Prof.Dogg's Troupe; Harriet Powell; A & C Black
The Happy Hedgehog Band; Martin Waddell; Barefoot Books
The Singing Sack: 28 Song-stories from Around the World; Helen East; A&C Black
Doing the Animal Bop (with CD); Lindsey Gardiner; Barron's Educational Series
The Big Book of Music Games; Debra Olsen Pressnall; Instructional Fair
High Low Dolly Pepper: Developing Basic Music Skills with Young Children; Veronica Clark; A&C Black

Curriculum coverage grid overleaf

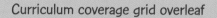

Potential NC KS1 Curriculum Coverage through the provocations suggested for sound and music.

Full version of KS1 PoS on pages 69-74
Photocopiable version on page 8

Literacy

	Lit 1 speak	Lit 2 listen	Lit 3 group	Lit 4 drama	Lit 5 word	Lit 6 spell	Lit 7 text1	Lit 8 text2	Lit 9 text3	Lit10 text4	Lit11 sentence	Lit12 presentation
Literacy	1.1	2.1	3.1	4.1	5.1	6.1	7.1	8.1	9.1	10.1	11.1	12.1
	1.2	2.2	3.2	4.2	5.2	6.2	7.2	8.2	9.2	10.2	11.2	12.2

Numeracy

	Num 1 U&A	Num 2 count	Num 3 number	Num 4 calculate	Num 5 shape	Num 6 measure	Num 7 data
Numeracy	1.1	2.1	3.1	4.1	5.1	6.1	7.1
	1.2	2.2	3.2	4.2	5.2	6.2	7.2

Science

	SC1 Enquiry			SC2 Life processes					SC3 Materials		SC4 Phys processes		
	Sc1.1	Sc1.2	Sc1.3	Sc2.1	Sc2.2	Sc2.3	Sc2.4	Sc2.5	Sc3.1	Sc3.2	Sc4.1	Sc4.2	Sc4.3
Science	1.1a	1.2a	1.3a	2.1a	2.2a	2.3a	2.4a	2.5a	3.1a	3.2a	4.1a	4.2a	4.3a
	1.1b	1.2b	1.3b	2.1b	2.2b	2.3b	2.4b	2.5b	3.1b	3.2b	4.1b	4.2b	4.3b
	1.1c	1.2c	1.3c	2.1c	2.2c	2.3c		2.5c	3.1c		4.1c	4.2c	4.3c
	1.1d				2.2d				3.1d				4.3d
					2.2e								
					2.2f								
					2.2g								

ICT

	ICT 1 finding out		ICT 2 ideas	ICT 3 reviewing	ICT 4 breadth
ICT	1.1a	1.2a	2a	3a	4a
	1.1b	1.2b	2b	3b	4b
	1.1c	1.2c	2c	3c	4c
		1.2d			

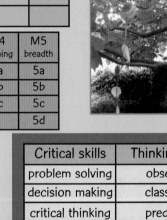

History

	H1 chronology	H2 events, people	H3 interpret	H4 enquire	H5 org & comm	H6 breadth
History	1a	2a	3a	4a	5a	6a
	1b	2b		4b		6b
						6c
						6d

Geography

	G1.1 & G1.2 enquiry		G2 places	G3 processes	G4 environment	G5 breadth
Geography	1.1a	1.2a	2a	3a	4a	5a
	1.1b	1.2b	2b	3b	4b	5b
	1.1c	1.2c	2c			5c
	1.1d	1.2d	2d			5d
			2e			

D&T

	D&T 1 developing	D&T 2 tool use	D&T 3 evaluating	D&T 4 materials	D&T 5 breadth
D&T	1a	2a	3a	4a	5a
	1b	2b	3b	4b	5b
	1c	2c			5c
	1d	2d			
	1e	2e			

Music

	M1 performing	M2 composing	M3 appraising	M4 listening	M5 breadth
Music	1a	2a	3a	4a	5a
	1b	2b	3b	4b	5b
	1c			4c	5c
					5d

PHSE&C

	PSHEC1 conf & resp	PSHEC2 citizenship	PSHEC3 health	PSHEC4 relationships
PHSE & C	1a	2a	3a	4a
	1b	2b	3b	4b
	1c	2c	3c	4c
	1d	2d	3d	4d
	1e	2e	3e	4e
		2f	3f	
		2g	3g	
		2h		

Art & Design

	A&D1 ideas	A&D2 making	A&D3 evaluating	A&D4 materials	A&D5 breadth
Art& Design	1a	2a	3a	4a	5a
	1b	2b	3b	4b	5b
		2c		4c	5c
					5d

PE

	PE1 devel skills	PE2 apply skills	PE3 evaluate	PE4 fitness	PE5 breadth
PE	1a	2a	3a	4a	5a dance
	1b	2b	3b	4b	5b games
		2c	3c		5c gym

Critical skills	Thinking Skills
problem solving	observing
decision making	classifying
critical thinking	prediction
creative thinking	making inferences
communication	problem solving
organisation	drawing conclusions
management	
leadership	

Dance and Movement

Dance and Movement

Previous experience in the Foundation Stage.

Moving and dancing are part of the Early Years Foundation Stage curriculum. Children will probably have danced in free play as well as in adult led sessions. They will have responded to a range of stimuli such as:

* drapes, net and ribbons;
* scarves;
* elastic and lycra;
* balls, hoops and beanbags.

Their dances may have evolved around:

* stories and poems;
* pictures and photographs;
* seasonal themes;
* themes from nature;
* artefacts;

and been inspired by music from a wide range of cultures.

Pause for thought

In the early stages of working with these materials it is crucial to continue to observe the children. Only by doing this can you set developmentally appropriate challenges and provocations. The ideas listed here are offered as suggestions; the most exciting challenges will arise from children's own interests and motivations, which will only become apparent as you spend time with them, watching and joining them in their play. As you do this, you will be moving between the three interconnecting roles of observer, co-player, extender described below, and will be able to decide what you need to do next to take the learning forward.

The responsive adult (see page 5)

In three interconnecting roles, the responsive adult will be:

observer

* observing
* listening
* interpreting

co-player

* modelling
* playing alongside
* offering suggestions
* responding sensitively
* initiating with care!

extender

* discussing ideas
* sharing thinking
* modelling new skills
* asking open questions
* being an informed extender
* instigating ideas & thoughts
* supporting children as they make links in learning
* making possibilities evident
* introducing new ideas and resources
* offering challenges and provocations

Offering Challenges and Provocations - some ideas:

In most cases, if children are to be involved in choreographing their own dances, they will first need experience of the process in adult modelled and adult supported sessions. Once this has happened, as long as they have access to the materials they need, and time to get involved, children will practise and extend what they have learned.

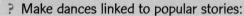

? Make dances linked to popular stories:
* Where the Wild Things are
* Funny Bones
* The Hungry Caterpillar
* Rainbow Fish.

? Create dances with ribbons and streamers, exploring different pathways and levels:
* zig-zags
* curved lines and swooping arcs
* straight lines and sharp turns
* high and low levels
* backwards and forwards.

? How might the dance look different if you use drapes, scarves or 'cheer-leader pompoms'?

? Find out all you can about these sorts of dancing:
* Bangra dancing
* line dancing
* square dancing
* maypole dancing
* barn dancing
* Scottish or Irish dancing
* Greek dancing, Flamenco
* African, Australian and other national dances.

? Can you do these dances - Jive, Rock and Roll, Limbo, Salsa, ballroom, or find out how to do them? You could ask your parents and grandparents to show you, and then have a show!

Ready for more?

- Can you devise a dance for:
  - two people?
  - three people?
  - four people?
  - more than ten people?

- Get some lycra and sew it into cylinders. Get inside and see how many different shapes you can make as you move your body. Can you fit more than one person inside to make a better shape?

- Get a friend to take some photos of you as you make shapes in the lycra tube.

- Collect some movement words by looking in word books or on the internet. How many different ones can you find? make a list and pin it up so you can add more when you find them.

- Choose six of your words and join the movements together to make a movement sentence.

- Now make up lots more movement sentences. If you work in a group, you could have a narrator who says the words as you move.

- Make a performance area outside, and plan your own dance festival. Make invitations, tickets and programmes, make up some dances, and invite some people to come and see your festival.

- Look on the internet and in books for some movement games. Try some of these out. Make a collection or scrapbook of games for your class to play.

Materials, equipment suppliers, websites, books and other references

Try www.spacekraft.co.uk for ribbon sticks, 'body sox' lycra suits, latex tube band for group work, or make your own using lengths of ribbon from markets and florists, tied to green garden sticks, chopsticks or even pencils.

Make cheer leader pompoms from fabric or thin carrier bags, cut in strips and tied in the middle to make a ball. Look at www.sport-thieme.co.uk to see examples.

www.cheerleading.org.uk/schools - the UK cheerleader website - where you can download a free leaflet on starting cheerleading in your school!

www.novelties-direct.co.uk - has a great selection of pompoms at reasonable prices.

www.teachingideas.co.uk/music - gives some ideas for simple rhythm activities. www.nncc.org has more information on rhythm.

www.standards.dfes.gov.uk/pdf/primaryschemes - has the QCA scheme of work for a unit of work for Years 1/2 on 'feel the Pulse - Exploring Pulse and Rhythm'

For images of dance and dancers, try **Google Images**, 'children dancing' 'ribbon sticks' 'cheerleader' 'cheerleader pompoms'.

Some suitable **books to use with younger children** include:

Let's Go, Zudie-o: Creative Activities for Dance and Music (Book and CD); Helen MacGregor; A & C Black

Helping Young children with Steady Beat; Ros Bayley, Lynn Broadbent; Lawrence Educational

Steady Beat Songs; Ros Bayley; Lawrence Educational

101 Dance Games for Children: Fun & Creativity with Movement; Paul Rooyackers; Hunter House

101 More Dance Games; Paul Rooyackers ; Hunter House

101 Movement Games for Children; Huberta Wiertsema; Hunter House

101 Rhythm Instrument Activities For Young Children; Abigail Flesch Connors; Gryphon House

Dancing Around the World; Nicholas Brasch; Longman

Dance for Infants; Jim Hall, A&C Black

Curriculum coverage grid overleaf

Potential NC KS1 Curriculum Coverage through the provocations suggested for dance and movement.

Full version of KS1 PoS on pages 69-74
Photocopiable version on page 8

Literacy

	Lit 1 speak	Lit 2 listen	Lit 3 group	Lit 4 drama	Lit 5 word	Lit 6 spell	Lit 7 text1	Lit 8 text2	Lit 9 text3	Lit10 text4	Lit11 sentence	Lit12 presentation
Literacy	1.1	2.1	3.1	4.1	5.1	6.1	7.1	8.1	9.1	10.1	11.1	12.1
	1.2	2.2	3.2	4.2	5.2	6.2	7.2	8.2	9.2	10.2	11.2	12.2

Numeracy

	Num 1 U&A	Num 2 count	Num 3 number	Num 4 calculate	Num 5 shape	Num 6 measure	Num 7 data
Numeracy	1.1	2.1	3.1	4.1	5.1	6.1	7.1
	1.2	2.2	3.2	4.2	5.2	6.2	7.2

Science

	SC1 Enquiry			SC2 Life processes					SC3 Materials		SC4 Phys processes		
	Sc1.1	Sc1.2	Sc1.3	Sc2.1	Sc2.2	Sc2.3	Sc2.4	Sc2.5	Sc3.1	Sc3.2	Sc4.1	Sc4.2	Sc4.3
Science	1.1a	1.2a	1.3a	2.1a	2.2a	2.3a	2.4a	2.5a	3.1a	3.2a	4.1a	4.2a	4.3a
	1.1b	1.2b	1.3b	2.1b	2.2b	2.3b	2.4b	2.5b	3.1b	3.2b	4.1b	4.2b	4.3b
	1.1c	1.2c	1.3c	2.1c	2.2c	2.3c		2.5c	3.1c		4.1c	4.2c	4.3c
	1.1d				2.2d				3.1d				4.3d
					2.2e								
					2.2f								
					2.2g								

ICT

	ICT 1 finding out		ICT 2 ideas	ICT 3 reviewing	ICT 4 breadth
ICT	1.1a	1.2a	2a	3a	4a
	1.1b	1.2b	2b	3b	4b
	1.1c	1.2c	2c	3c	4c
		1.2d			

D&T

	D&T 1 developing	D&T 2 tool use	D&T 3 evaluating	D&T 4 materials	D&T 5 breadth
D&T	1a	2a	3a	4a	5a
	1b	2b	3b	4b	5b
	1c	2c			5c
	1d	2d			
	1e	2e			

History

	H1 chronology	H2 events, people	H3 interpret	H4 enquire	H5 org & comm	H6 breadth
History	1a	2a	3a	4a	5a	6a
	1b	2b		4b		6b
						6c
						6d

Geography

	G1.1 & G1.2 enquiry		G2 places	G3 processes	G4 environment	G5 breadth
Geography	1.1a	1.2a	2a	3a	4a	5a
	1.1b	1.2b	2b	3b	4b	5b
	1.1c	1.2c	2c			5c
	1.1d	1.2d	2d			5d
			2e			

Music

	M1 performing	M2 composing	M3 appraising	M4 listening	M5 breadth
Music	1a	2a	3a	4a	5a
	1b	2b	3b	4b	5b
	1c			4c	5c
					5d

PHSE & C

	PSHEC1 conf & resp	PSHEC2 citizenship	PSHEC3 health	PSHEC4 relationships
PHSE & C	1a	2a	3a	4a
	1b	2b	3b	4b
	1c	2c	3c	4c
	1d	2d	3d	4d
	1e	2e	3e	4e
		2f	3f	
		2g	3g	
		2h		

Art & Design

	A&D1 ideas	A&D2 making	A&D3 evaluating	A&D4 materials	A&D5 breadth
Art & Design	1a	2a	3a	4a	5a
	1b	2b	3b	4b	5b
		2c		4c	5c
					5d

PE

	PE1 devel skills	PE2 apply skills	PE3 evaluate	PE4 fitness	PE5 breadth
PE	1a	2a	3a	4a	5a dance
	1b	2b	3b	4b	5b games
		2c	3c		5c gym

Critical skills / Thinking Skills

Critical skills	Thinking Skills
problem solving	observing
decision making	classifying
critical thinking	prediction
creative thinking	making inferences
communication	problem solving
organisation	drawing conclusions
management	
leadership	

Minibeast

Previous experience in the Foundation Stage.
Experiencing living things is a key part of the early years curriculum, and a fascination with minibeasts is central to many children's interests. In the EYFS, children will probably have:

* watched and investigated minibeasts in gardens and outdoor spaces;
* used bug collectors and magnifying glasses;

and may also have:

* watched caterpillars turning into butterflies;
* made a wormery;
* made an ant farm;
* watched slugs and snails;
* gone on a minibeast hunt.

Pause for thought
In the early stages of working with these materials it is crucial to continue to observe the children. Only by doing this can you set developmentally appropriate challenges and provocations. The ideas listed here are offered as suggestions; the most exciting challenges will arise from children's own interests and motivations, which will only become apparent as you spend time with them, watching and joining them in their play. As you do this, you will be moving between the three interconnecting roles of observer, co-player, extender described below, and will be able to decide what you need to do next to take the learning forward.

The responsive adult (see page 5)

In three interconnecting roles, the responsive adult will be:

observer

* observing
* listening
* interpreting

co-player

* modelling
* playing alongside
* offering suggestions
* responding sensitively
* initiating with care!

extender

* discussing ideas
* sharing thinking
* modelling new skills
* asking open questions
* being an informed extender
* instigating ideas & thoughts
* supporting children as they make links in learning
* making possibilities evident
* introducing new ideas and resources
* offering challenges and provocations

Offering Challenges and Provocations - some ideas:

In KS1 children may need to top up their experiences of minibeasts with further use of magnifying glasses, bug collectors and time to watch minibeasts in action in your outdoor area. Then start with simple challenges that reinforce positive attitudes to living things, and care in handling equipment.

? Find a magnifying glass and a clip board. Now can you explore and record the names of the living things that live in your outside area?

? Can you find some snails or slugs? Gently collect some and put them in an aquarium or a big plastic box. Watch what they do. can you give them something they would like to eat? Find out what they need by looking in books or the internet. Put the creatures back where you found them after you have looked at them.

? Make an information book or poster about minibeasts that live in your school grounds. Use a camera, draw pictures or find some pictures on the internet.

? Work with some friends to look under stones and logs for very small insects, flies and beetles. Collect some and make a habitat for them in a plastic box. Handle them gently, and don't forget to look at where they were living, so you make the right sort of habitat.

? Put one of these words in Google Images 'minibeasts' 'caterpillars' 'slugs' 'butterflies' 'moths' 'spiders' and find out all you can about the minibeast of your choice.

? Make a minibeast quiz for your friends. Choose or draw some pictures of minibeasts and stick them on cards. Now challenge your friends to name them. You could make a game of Minibeast Snap, Minibeast Pairs or Minibeast Bingo.

? Make a habitat for Spiderman that will attract spiders. You need to think hard about what spiders like and where they live.

Ready for more?

- Work with some friends to make a minibeast habitat in your garden or school grounds. Research what to do by contacting local environmental groups, who may come to help you. Then look at the sort of minibeasts that live in your grounds and choose materials for their habitat that they will like. You can use stones, concrete slabs, guttering, wood, logs, sticks, leaves, moss and many other natural and man-made materials. Take some photos of the habitat as you build it, and then record the minibeasts that visit.

- Make a powerpoint presentation of the photos of your habitat, and show the presentation to your friends, other classes, parents and even the whole school!

- Find out about how minibeasts reproduce. Do they lay eggs? If so, what do they look like and where could you find some? What to baby minibeasts look like? Which ones look like their parents and which ones have to change as they grow. What do baby minibeasts eat?

- Find out how to make an ant farm or a wormery, then make one for your classroom. <u>Collect all the things you need, including a good container before you collect the ants or worms</u>.

- Send for a butterfly box from www.greengardener.co.uk and grow your own butterflies from caterpillars.

Materials, equipment suppliers, websites, books and other references

Some ideas for **resources and equipment**:

Educational suppliers have plenty of science resources that are ideal for minibeast work. Make sure you have plenty of magnifying glasses, bug boxes and collecting devices. you also need some plastic aquariums, and plastic boxes of all sizes. Store these somewhere accessible so children can get them easily as they work. You could also add some replica minibeasts that can be offered in small containers or baskets to inspire stories and environments - include insects, beetles, ants etc.

There are hundreds of **minibeast sites and images** on the internet, and these have downloadable leaflets of ideas and information, some for children, some for teachers: www.ers.north-ayrshire.gov.uk/minibeasts www.highlandschools-virtualib.org.uk tre.ngfl.gov.uk (Teacher Resource exchange) www.ehsni.gov.uk - environmental heritage site with booklets to download www.nwt.org.uk - for a Minibeasts.pdf leaflet www.ypte.org.uk/docs/factsheets/env_facts/minibeasts - Young People's Trust for the Environment with good information and activities www.bbsrc.ac.uk/society/schools/primary/minibeast/discovery2.pdf - a leaflet on Making Bug boxes www.sutton.gov.uk or www.ntseducation.org.uk - for minibeast workpacks. www.insectlore.co.uk have butterfly kits and lots of other insect resources and information about keeping and investigating insects, and web.ukonline.co.uk/conker/pond-dip/tadpoles - has information on keeping tadpoles. These are just a few!

Books and Publications:

Minibeasts (Amazing Life Cycles); George McGavin; ticktock Media Ltd
Minibeasts (Foundations); Rachel Sparks-Linfield; A & C Black
Minibeasts; Siobhan Hardy; Collins Educational
Minibeasts (Hot Topics); Gerald Legg; Belitha Press Ltd
Slugs and Snails (Minibeasts); Claire Llewellyn; Franklin Watts
Spiders, Insects, and Minibeasts (Scary Creatures); Penny Clarke; Franklin Watts
Minibeasts (poems); Brian Moses; Macmillan Children's Books
Outdoor Fun and Games for Kids: Over 100 Activities for 3-11 Year Olds; Jane Kemp; Hamlyn
Outdoor Activities for Kids: Over 100, Practical Things to Do Outside; Clare Bradley; Lorenz Books
The Kid's Wildlife Book: Exploring Animal Worlds; Williamson Publishing
From Tadpole to Frog; Wendy Pfeffer; Harper Trophy
From Caterpillar to Butterfly; Deborah Heiligman; Harper Collins
The Very Hungry Caterpillar; Eric Carle; Picture Puffin

Curriculum coverage grid overleaf

Potential NC KS1 Curriculum Coverage through the provocations suggested for minibeast.

Full version of KS1 PoS on pages 69-74
Photocopiable version on page 8

Literacy

	Lit 1 speak	Lit 2 listen	Lit 3 group	Lit 4 drama	Lit 5 word	Lit 6 spell	Lit 7 text1	Lit 8 text2	Lit 9 text3	Lit10 text4	Lit11 sentence	Lit12 presentation
Literacy	1.1	2.1	3.1	4.1	5.1	6.1	7.1	8.1	9.1	10.1	11.1	12.1
	1.2	2.2	3.2	4.2	5.2	6.2	7.2	8.2	9.2	10.2	11.2	12.2

Numeracy

	Num 1 U&A	Num 2 count	Num 3 number	Num 4 calculate	Num 5 shape	Num 6 measure	Num 7 data
Numeracy	1.1	2.1	3.1	4.1	5.1	6.1	7.1
	1.2	2.2	3.2	4.2	5.2	6.2	7.2

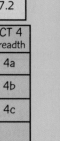

Science

	SC1 Enquiry			SC2 Life processes					SC3 Materials		SC4 Phys processes		
	Sc1.1	Sc1.2	Sc1.3	Sc2.1	Sc2.2	Sc2.3	Sc2.4	Sc2.5	Sc3.1	Sc3.2	Sc4.1	Sc4.2	Sc4.3
Science	1.1a	1.2a	1.3a	2.1a	2.2a	2.3a	2.4a	2.5a	3.1a	3.2a	4.1a	4.2a	4.3a
	1.1b	1.2b	1.3b	2.1b	2.2b	2.3b	2.4b	2.5b	3.1b	3.2b	4.1b	4.2b	4.3b
	1.1c	1.2c	1.3c	2.1c	2.2c	2.3c		2.5c	3.1c		4.1c	4.2c	4.3c
	1.1d				2.2d				3.1d				4.3d
					2.2e								
					2.2f								
					2.2g								

ICT

	ICT 1 finding out		ICT 2 ideas	ICT 3 reviewing	ICT 4 breadth
	1.1a	1.2a	2a	3a	4a
ICT	1.1b	1.2b	2b	3b	4b
	1.1c	1.2c	2c	3c	4c
		1.2d			

D&T

	D&T 1 developing	D&T 2 tool use	D&T 3 evaluating	D&T 4 materials	D&T 5 breadth
	1a	2a	3a	4a	5a
D&T	1b	2b	3b	4b	5b
	1c	2c			5c
	1d	2d			
	1e	2e			

History

	H1 chronology	H2 events, people	H3 interpret	H4 enquire	H5 org & comm	H6 breadth
	1a	2a	3a	4a	5a	6a
History	1b	2b		4b		6b
						6c
						6d

Geography

	G1.1 & G1.2 enquiry		G2 places	G3 processes	G4 environment	G5 breadth
	1.1a	1.2a	2a	3a	4a	5a
Geography	1.1b	1.2b	2b	3b	4b	5b
	1.1c	1.2c	2c			5c
	1.1d	1.2d	2d			5d
			2e			

Music

	M1 performing	M2 composing	M3 appraising	M4 listening	M5 breadth
	1a	2a	3a	4a	5a
Music	1b	2b	3b	4b	5b
	1c			4c	5c
					5d

PHSE & C

	PSHEC1 conf & resp	PSHEC2 citizenship	PSHEC3 health	PSHEC4 relationships
	1a	2a	3a	4a
	1b	2b	3b	4b
PHSE & C	1c	2c	3c	4c
	1d	2d	3d	4d
	1e	2e	3e	4e
		2f	3f	
		2g	3g	
		2h		

Art & Design

	A&D1 ideas	A&D2 making	A&D3 evaluating	A&D4 materials	A&D5 breadth
	1a	2a	3a	4a	5a
Art & Design	1b	2b	3b	4b	5b
		2c		4c	5c
					5d

PE

	PE1 devel skills	PE2 apply skills	PE3 evaluate	PE4 fitness	PE5 breadth
	1a	2a	3a	4a	5a dance
PE	1b	2b	3b	4b	5b games
		2c	3c		5c gym

Critical skills	Thinking Skills
problem solving	observing
decision making	classifying
critical thinking	prediction
creative thinking	making inferences
communication	problem solving
organisation	drawing conclusions
management	
leadership	

Growing Things

Growing Things

Previous experience in the Foundation Stage.

Growing seeds, bulbs and plants is a part of every early years setting, and children should be familiar with digging, planting, growing and tending plants through some of these activities:

* digging activities in mud and compost;
* using simple tools and equipment
* planting and growing seeds such as beans and flowers;
* planting young plants in window boxes and tubs for decoration;
* growing simple food plants such as beans, lettuce, cress, tomatoes;
* growing bulbs indoors and outside;
* making and playing in sensory gardens;
* making gardens or helping to plant living willow or other garden plants for play and decoration.

Pause for thought

In the early stages of working with these materials it is crucial to continue to observe the children. Only by doing this can you set developmentally appropriate challenges and provocations. The ideas listed here are offered as suggestions; the most exciting challenges will arise from children's own interests and motivations, which will only become apparent as you spend time with them, watching and joining them in their play. As you do this, you will be moving between the three interconnecting roles of observer, co-player, extender described below, and will be able to decide what you need to do next to take the learning forward.

The responsive adult (see page 5)

In three interconnecting roles, the responsive adult will be:

* observing
* listening
* interpreting

observer

* modelling
* playing alongside
* offering suggestions
* responding sensitively
* initiating with care!

co-player

* discussing ideas
* sharing thinking
* modelling new skills
* asking open questions
* being an informed extender
* instigating ideas & thoughts
* supporting children as they make links in learning
* making possibilities evident
* introducing new ideas and resources
* offering challenges and provocations

extender

Offering Challenges and Provocations - some ideas:

Growing plants is a good way to encourage pride in the school environment and to help develop a sense of responsibility. Children can be involved in small and larger projects from planting sunflowers to redesigning the whole school garden or making a forest school area. here are some simple starters for independent work.

? Go for a walk in your school garden or grounds and take photos of all the different plants you see. Some of these may be weeds. When you have downloaded or printed your photos, use the library or the internet to find out what they are.

? Collect some seeds and pips from fruit and vegetables - apple and orange pips, tomato pips, melon seeds, avocado stones, anything you eat. Now collect some simple containers such as yogurt pots or plastic cups and try growing some of your seeds. They may take a long time to start growing, so be patient and find out how to look after them.

? While you are waiting for your seeds and pips to grow, design a plant pot, using a plastic pot and recycled materials.

? Look round your outdoor area and see if there are some places where you could grow plants for flowers or food. make a plan, draw your ideas and see if your teachers can help you to grow some.

? Are there any trees in your school grounds? Photograph these and find out their names. Make a book for the school library with all the school trees in it.

? Get some sunflower seeds and grow them. Have a contest to see who can grow the tallest one. When they have flowered, keep the seeds to feed the birds.

? Get some bulbs (if you buy them near Christmas, they will be cheaper!). Grow them in your classroom for flowers in the spring.

Ready for more?

- Find out about Living Willow by looking on the internet at www.livingwillow.fsnet.co.uk. Can you think of a way to raise some money to plant living willow in your school grounds?

- In the autumn, go outside and see how many different kinds of seeds you can find. Collect them in bags and label the bags, so you don't forget what they are. Now plant the seeds in different pots and see what grows.

- Get some plastic pots, a growbag and some vegetable seeds. What do you need to do to make a vegetable garden?

- can you make a scarecrow for your garden, to stop the birds from eating your seeds? Collect some recycled materials and have a scarecrow competition to see who can make the best one.

- Find some old, clean towels and cut them up to fit in shallow containers. Make the towelling wet. Now sprinkle some of these seeds on the damp towelling - grass seed, cress, mustard, nasturtiums, peas. Watch what happens, taking photos every two days. Make a display of your experiments.

- Can you make a hanging basket from recycled materials? Look for some young plants - pansies, petunias, geraniums, lobelia etc to plant in your hanging basket. After the summer, plant your basket again with bulbs, winter pansies or herbs for the winter.

Materials, equipment suppliers, websites, books and other references

Suppliers of equipment and resources:

Strong tools are essential for school use - invest in some good ones specially made for children www.brio.co.uk will give you stockists. Or buy small versions of adult tools (usually labelled for women!). More and more of the educational suppliers are stocking garden tools, so check these or your local consortium group for prices. TTS Group www.tts-group.co.uk have a range of tools and barrows etc.

Ask parents and friends for used plant pots, plant saucers and other recycled materials. They may also be willing to donate excess seedlings and cuttings from plants. Grow bags are a cheap way of gardening with children (choose ones with contents from sustainable sources). Provide a digging area if you can, where children can explore the fun of just digging.

Try **Google** to find out about plants and flowers, and don't forget that some weeds have lovely flowers and leaves, and are also free. Find out about quick growing and child friendly plants from the Royal Horticultural Society www.rhs.org.uk and click on 'plant finder'. The BBC www.bbc.co.uk - has a Gardening with Children section.
www.sustainweb.org - growing plants (planting seeds such as fruit pips and stones
www.standards.dfes.gov.uk/schemes2/science - DfES guidance on growing things
www-saps.plantsci.cam.ac.uk - download leaflet on growing seeds
www.naturegrid.org.uk - QCA ideas on growing things
www.thekidsgarden.co.uk - recycling for kids
or try www.ltl.org.uk - the Learning Through Landscapes website

The Little Book of Growing Things (from www.featherstone.uk.com) has hundreds of ideas for school gardening, many of them free or cheap options.

Some Books:
Nature's Playground; Fiona Danks; Frances Lincoln Publishers
Great Gardens for Kids; Clare Matthews; Hamlyn
Gardening with Children; Kim Wilde; Collins
Harry's Garden; Kim Wilde; Collins Educational
How To Make a Scarecrow; Kim Wilde; Collins Educational
Roots, Shoots, Buckets and Boots; Sharon Lovejoy; Workman
Usborne Starting Gardening; Sue Johnson; E.D.C. Publishing
The Gardening Book; Jane Bull; Dorling Kindersley

Curriculum coverage grid overleaf

Potential NC KS1 Curriculum Coverage through the provocations suggested for growing things.

Literacy

	Lit 1 speak	Lit 2 listen	Lit 3 group	Lit 4 drama	Lit 5 word	Lit 6 spell	Lit 7 text1	Lit 8 text2	Lit 9 text3	Lit10 text4	Lit11 sentence	Lit12 presentation
Literacy	1.1	2.1	3.1	4.1	5.1	6.1	7.1	8.1	9.1	10.1	11.1	12.1
	1.2	2.2	3.2	4.2	5.2	6.2	7.2	8.2	9.2	10.2	11.2	12.2

Numeracy

	Num 1 U&A	Num 2 count	Num 3 number	Num 4 calculate	Num 5 shape	Num 6 measure	Num 7 data
Numeracy	1.1	2.1	3.1	4.1	5.1	6.1	7.1
	1.2	2.2	3.2	4.2	5.2	6.2	7.2

Full version of KS1 PoS on pages 69-74
Photocopiable version on page 8

Science

	SC1 Enquiry			SC2 Life processes					SC3 Materials		SC4 Phys processes		
	Sc1.1	Sc1.2	Sc1.3	Sc2.1	Sc2.2	Sc2.3	Sc2.4	Sc2.5	Sc3.1	Sc3.2	Sc4.1	Sc4.2	Sc4.3
Science	1.1a	1.2a	1.3a	2.1a	2.2a	2.3a	2.4a	2.5a	3.1a	3.2a	4.1a	4.2a	4.3a
	1.1b	1.2b	1.3b	2.1b	2.2b	2.3b	2.4b	2.5b	3.1b	3.2b	4.1b	4.2b	4.3b
	1.1c	1.2c	1.3c	2.1c	2.2c	2.3c		2.5c	3.1c		4.1c	4.2c	4.3c
	1.1d				2.2d				3.1d				4.3d
					2.2e								
					2.2f								
					2.2g								

ICT

	ICT 1 finding out		ICT 2 ideas	ICT 3 reviewing	ICT 4 breadth
ICT	1.1a	1.2a	2a	3a	4a
	1.1b	1.2b	2b	3b	4b
	1.1c	1.2c	2c	3c	4c
		1.2d			

D&T

	D&T 1 developing	D&T 2 tool use	D&T 3 evaluating	D&T 4 materials	D&T 5 breadth
D&T	1a	2a	3a	4a	5a
	1b	2b	3b	4b	5b
	1c	2c			5c
	1d	2d			
	1e	2e			

History

	H1 chronology	H2 events, people	H3 interpret	H4 enquire	H5 org & comm	H6 breadth
History	1a	2a	3a	4a	5a	6a
	1b	2b		4b		6b
						6c
						6d

Geography

	G1.1 & G1.2 enquiry		G2 places	G3 processes	G4 environment	G5 breadth
Geography	1.1a	1.2a	2a	3a	4a	5a
	1.1b	1.2b	2b	3b	4b	5b
	1.1c	1.2c	2c			5c
	1.1d	1.2d	2d			5d
			2e			

Music

	M1 performing	M2 composing	M3 appraising	M4 listening	M5 breadth
Music	1a	2a	3a	4a	5a
	1b	2b	3b	4b	5b
	1c			4c	5c
					5d

PHSE & C

	PSHEC1 conf & resp	PSHEC2 citizenship	PSHEC3 health	PSHEC4 relationships
PHSE & C	1a	2a	3a	4a
	1b	2b	3b	4b
	1c	2c	3c	4c
	1d	2d	3d	4d
	1e	2e	3e	4e
		2f	3f	
		2g	3g	
		2h		

Art & Design

	A&D1 ideas	A&D2 making	A&D3 evaluating	A&D4 materials	A&D5 breadth
Art & Design	1a	2a	3a	4a	5a
	1b	2b	3b	4b	5b
		2c		4c	5c
					5d

PE

	PE1 devel skills	PE2 apply skills	PE3 evaluate	PE4 fitness	PE5 breadth
PE	1a	2a	3a	4a	5a dance
	1b	2b	3b	4b	5b games
		2c	3c		5c gym

Critical skills	Thinking Skills
problem solving	observing
decision making	classifying
critical thinking	prediction
creative thinking	making inferences
communication	problem solving
organisation	drawing conclusions
management	
leadership	

Mark Making and Writing

Mark making & writing

Previous experience in the Foundation Stage.
By the time they reach Year 1, most children will have had extensive opportunities to use mark making materials for a wide range of purposes and in many different contexts. They will have made marks with everything from fingers and toes to water colour crayons as part of:

* role play;
* activities in a graphics area;
* out of doors in gardens and other spaces;
* in construction;
* when working with clay, dough and other malleable materials;
* free play on a range of surfaces;
* playing in mud, water, snow;
* making signs, notices and labels;
* making messages and writing letters.

Pause for thought

In the early stages of working with these materials it is crucial to continue to observe the children. Only by doing this can you set developmentally appropriate challenges and provocations. The ideas listed here are offered as suggestions; the most exciting challenges will arise from children's own interests and motivations, which will only become apparent as you spend time with them, watching and joining them in their play. As you do this, you will be moving between the three interconnecting roles of observer, co-player, extender described below, and will be able to decide what you need to do next to take the learning forward.

The responsive adult (see page 5)

In three interconnecting roles, the responsive adult will be:

* observing
* listening
* interpreting

observer

* modelling
* playing alongside
* offering suggestions
* responding sensitively
* initiating with care!

co-player

* discussing ideas
* sharing thinking
* modelling new skills
* asking open questions
* being an informed extender
* instigating ideas & thoughts
* supporting children as they make links in learning
* making possibilities evident
* introducing new ideas and resources
* offering challenges and provocations

extender

Offering Challenges and Provocations - some ideas:

NOTE: Portable mark-making kits make it much easier for children to draw and write outside, in places of their own choice, and they are particularly attractive to boys. Replenish these kits regularly with attractive and colourful materials to stimulate children's imaginations. The kits can be used for both adult led and child initiated activities, while children are:

* role-playing - to develop and record narratives, or to make maps and signs
* constructing - to make plans, write lists and instructions
* investigating - to record experiments, collect information
* being creative - in making marks of all sorts
* practising and extending what they are learning in the classroom (see photo).

? Can you plan and set up a Treasure Hunt for your friends? You could bury treasure in sand, or make a treasure hunt round the whole outdoor area. Plan your Treasure Hunt first, then write the instructions for your friends to follow. See if you can hide each clue in a different place.

? Can you lay a trail with chalk for your friends to follow? Make marks or arrows on the ground or on walls, paths and fences. Give yourself a five minute start before they follow you!

? Make a notice board for your outside area or the playground. Hang it on a fence or wall, and use chalk, pencil or felt pens to write messages for your friends. You could announce a play or parade, invite them to play a game with you, or leave a message in code or secret writing.

? Look up 'prayer flags' in Google Images. Can you make some flags with writing or messages on them. You will need some strips of fabric and some paint. Old sheets make good flags if your tear them in strips. You could start by making name flags for everyone in your class.

Ready for more?

🖐 Make some posters about the animals, birds, minibeasts and plants in your school garden or outdoor area. Can you find a way of making your posters waterproof, so they can be displayed outside?

🖐 Find a notebook or diary and use this to make an Outdoor Diary of the school play area or garden. Take turns to write and draw about the things you see. You could include:

- the weather
- birds, insects and animals you see
- plants, flowers, leaves
- sounds you hear
- the clouds
- signs of the seasons
- the sorts of games you played
- photos as well as drawings.

🖐 Make a collection of weather and wildlife poems. You could start with some from books and the internet, and then write some more of your own.

🖐 Can you design and make a book of games that can be played outside? Start with the ones you know, then ask your family and friends if they know any more.

🖐 Can you be a pavement artist and make a picture on the path, playground or patio? Use chalk and make sure you do it where you will not be walked on!

🖐 Find a camera and use it to help you make an outdoor alphabet book with photos and words. Design a good cover for your book.

Materials, equipment suppliers, websites, books and other references

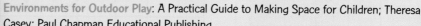

Try www.newitts.com - for playground chalk, cones and markers for games.
www.scienceyear.com/under11s/playground - and download a free leaflet with ideas for painting your own playground games
www.playquest.co.uk - make playground markings and have some good ideas in the photos on their website, as well as giant chess and draught pieces
www.linepainting.net - more ideas for markings
www.pioneer.cwc.net/playgroundpals.htm - takes you to a whole list of sites with ideas for playground games
www.worcestershire.gov.uk/home/09_play_mark.pdf - to download a free leaflet on making playground markings
www.sunclocks.com - for some pictures of paintings on a playground

Try Google Images: 'pavement art' 'graffiti' 'mural' 'pavement art'.

Look at users.skynet.be/J.Beever/pave.htm for some amazing 3D pavement drawings.

Download a really nice guide to making nature notebooks from www.nwf.org/kidzone

Some Books about outdoor environments:

Environments for Outdoor Play: A Practical Guide to Making Space for Children; Theresa Casey; Paul Chapman Educational Publishing

Ecoart!: Earth-friendly Art and Craft Experiences for 3 to 9 Year Olds; Lauri Carlson; Williamson Publishing

Playing Outside; Helen Bilton; David Fulton Publishers

Outdoor Play in the Early Years; Helen Bilton; David Fulton Publishers

Creating a Space to Grow; Gail Ryder-Richardson; David Fulton Publishers

Playing and Learning Outdoors; Jan White; Routledge

Sidewalk Chalk: Outdoor Fun and Games; Jamie Kyle McGillian; Sterling Juvenile

A Piece of Chalk; Jennifer A. Ericsson; Roaring Brook Press

Squeaky Chalk; Joy Sikorski; Random House

The Jumbo Book of Outdoor Art; Irene Luxbacher; Kids Can Press

The Little Book of Writing and The Little Book of Props for Writing; Featherstone Education

Curriculum coverage grid overleaf

Potential NC KS1 Curriculum Coverage through the provocations suggested for mark making and writing.

Full version of KS1 PoS on pages 69-74
Photocopiable version on page 8

Literacy

	Lit 1 speak	Lit 2 listen	Lit 3 group	Lit 4 drama	Lit 5 word	Lit 6 spell	Lit 7 text1	Lit 8 text2	Lit 9 text3	Lit10 text4	Lit11 sentence	Lit12 presentation
Literacy	1.1	2.1	3.1	4.1	5.1	6.1	7.1	8.1	9.1	10.1	11.1	12.1
	1.2	2.2	3.2	4.2	5.2	6.2	7.2	8.2	9.2	10.2	11.2	12.2

Numeracy

	Num 1 U&A	Num 2 count	Num 3 number	Num 4 calculate	Num 5 shape	Num 6 measure	Num 7 data
Numeracy	1.1	2.1	3.1	4.1	5.1	6.1	7.1
	1.2	2.2	3.2	4.2	5.2	6.2	7.2

Science

	SC1 Enquiry			SC2 Life processes					SC3 Materials		SC4 Phys processes		
	Sc1.1	Sc1.2	Sc1.3	Sc2.1	Sc2.2	Sc2.3	Sc2.4	Sc2.5	Sc3.1	Sc3.2	Sc4.1	Sc4.2	Sc4.3
Science	1.1a	1.2a	1.3a	2.1a	2.2a	2.3a	2.4a	2.5a	3.1a	3.2a	4.1a	4.2a	4.3a
	1.1b	1.2b	1.3b	2.1b	2.2b	2.3b	2.4b	2.5b	3.1b	3.2b	4.1b	4.2b	4.3b
	1.1c	1.2c	1.3c	2.1c	2.2c	2.3c		2.5c	3.1c		4.1c	4.2c	4.3c
	1.1d				2.2d				3.1d				4.3d
					2.2e								
					2.2f								
					2.2g								

ICT

	ICT 1 finding out		ICT 2 ideas	ICT 3 reviewing	ICT 4 breadth
ICT	1.1a	1.2a	2a	3a	4a
	1.1b	1.2b	2b	3b	4b
	1.1c	1.2c	2c	3c	4c
		1.2d			

D&T

	D&T 1 developing	D&T 2 tool use	D&T 3 evaluating	D&T 4 materials	D&T 5 breadth
D&T	1a	2a	3a	4a	5a
	1b	2b	3b	4b	5b
	1c	2c			5c
	1d	2d			
	1e	2e			

History

	H1 chronology	H2 events, people	H3 interpret	H4 enquire	H5 org & comm	H6 breadth
History	1a	2a	3a	4a	5a	6a
	1b	2b		4b		6b
						6c
						6d

Geography

	G1.1 & G1.2 enquiry		G2 places	G3 processes	G4 environment	G5 breadth
Geography	1.1a	1.2a	2a	3a	4a	5a
	1.1b	1.2b	2b	3b	4b	5b
	1.1c	1.2c	2c			5c
	1.1d	1.2d	2d			5d
			2e			

Music

	M1 performing	M2 composing	M3 appraising	M4 listening	M5 breadth
Music	1a	2a	3a	4a	5a
	1b	2b	3b	4b	5b
	1c			4c	5c
					5d

PHSE & C

	PSHEC1 conf & resp	PSHEC2 citizenship	PSHEC3 health	PSHEC4 relationships
PHSE & C	1a	2a	3a	4a
	1b	2b	3b	4b
	1c	2c	3c	4c
	1d	2d	3d	4d
	1e	2e	3e	4e
		2f	3f	
		2g	3g	
		2h		

Art & Design

	A&D1 ideas	A&D2 making	A&D3 evaluating	A&D4 materials	A&D5 breadth
Art & Design	1a	2a	3a	4a	5a
	1b	2b	3b	4b	5b
		2c		4c	5c
					5d

PE

	PE1 devel skills	PE2 apply skills	PE3 evaluate	PE4 fitness	PE5 breadth
PE	1a	2a	3a	4a	5a dance
	1b	2b	3b	4b	5b games
		2c	3c		5c gym

Critical skills	Thinking Skills
problem solving	observing
decision making	classifying
critical thinking	prediction
creative thinking	making inferences
communication	problem solving
organisation	drawing conclusions
management	
leadership	

Dens and Shelters

Dens and Drapes

Previous experience in the Foundation Stage.

Making dens is a favourite occupation for children in Nursery and Reception. Most children will have had experience of using drapes, sticks, pegs and other things to make dens in the gardens of their settings:

* under climbing fames;
* against walls;
* under trees, in in bushes and hedges;
* in tents and under clothes airer;

they will also have used drapes for

* dressing up;
* wrapping themselves and other objects;
* making tents, wigwams, houses;
* dancing;
* using drapes as a home-made parachute.

Pause for thought

In the early stages of working with these materials it is crucial to continue to observe the children. Only by doing this can you set developmentally appropriate challenges and provocations. The ideas listed here are offered as suggestions; the most exciting challenges will arise from children's own interests and motivations, which will only become apparent as you spend time with them, watching and joining them in their play. As you do this, you will be moving between the three interconnecting roles of observer, co-player, extender described below, and will be able to decide what you need to do next to take the learning forward.

The responsive adult (see page 5)

In three interconnecting roles, the responsive adult will be:

* observing
* listening
* interpreting

* modelling
* playing alongside
* offering suggestions
* responding sensitively
* initiating with care!

* discussing ideas
* sharing thinking
* modelling new skills
* asking open questions
* being an informed extender
* instigating ideas & thoughts
* supporting children as they make links in learning
* making possibilities evident
* introducing new ideas and resources
* offering challenges and provocations

Offering Challenges and Provocations - some ideas:

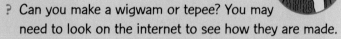

NOTE: Offer all sorts of den building materials to the children - canes, sticks, fabrics (lightweight ones are easiest to manage), clips and pegs, string and rope, boxes and cardboard.

? Can you make a wigwam or tepee? You may need to look on the internet to see how they are made.
? Can you make a shelter with:
  * three vertical sides?
  * four sloping sides?
  * six triangular sides?
? Can you make a den from branches, sticks and leaves?
? Can you make a den from boxes? Can you make it waterproof and windproof? Take some photos to show what you did. Make a display of your photos.
? Put 'building dens' in Google Images for some ideas.
? Can you make a den for an animal? Look on Google 'animal dens'.
? Can you make a den from sticks and plastic? Take care when you are using plastic. Can you make the den so dark that you can use a torch inside?
? Get some plain fabric (old sheets are good for this, so ask your parents if they have any). Now decorate the fabric before you make a 'designer den' with it. You could use:
  * felt pens
  * fabric crayons
  * tie dye
  * printing with objects
  * spray painting with dilute food colouring and hand sprays
  * sticking on patches of different fabrics, natural objects such as leaves, or buttons, sequins and beads.
? Can you find two points outside where you could tie the ends of a rope? If you can, try making a den by draping a big sheet or blanket over the rope and putting stones on the edges to keep the tent open.

Ready for more?

- Make a den from plastic carrier bags. Can you think of a way to fix the bags together? You could use:
  - Gaffer (silver duct) tape
  - brown parcel tape
  - a big needle and thread
  - staples.

  Which works best? Work in groups to trial and evaluate each method.

- What makes the best framework for a den? Is it:
  - canes?
  - branches?
  - broom handles?

  Which works best?

- Can you make a wind-proof AND water-proof den?

- Can you make a den with more than one room? Is it big enough for furniture?

- Look at how a pop-up tent is made. Can you make a den using the same method? What could you use?

- Can you make a shelter from recycled materials? Look at the photo, on the bottom right, of a shelter made from empty plastic bottles. Can you see how it is made?

- Use the internet to find out about Living Willow and how you can plant a living willow den. Could you plant one in your school garden or grounds?

- This picture is a den in some woods that was made by grown-ups. What do you think it is for? Can you guess?

Materials, equipment suppliers, websites, books and other references

Children need lots of flexible resources to make dens and shelters, and many of these are cheap or even free. Try collecting some of these:

- sticks, canes and bamboo;
- cable ties, string, tape of all sorts;
- fabric sheets (lightweight ones such as sheeting or sari fabric work well);
- pegs, clips, elastic, hair 'scrunchies';
- plastic sheeting (such as cheap dust-sheets), light tarpaulins, bubble wrap;
- plastic carrier bags and bin bags;
- cardboard boxes;
- cardboard sheeting from the sides of boxes and cartons;

Ask parents and local businesses to help by offering you packaging materials.

Google Images 'tree house' for some staggering examples, or 'den' 'hut' 'house in the woods' 'kids playhouse' 'nest'.

Books and Stories:

The Best Den Ever; Anne Cassidy; Franklin Watts

Children's Special Places: Exploring the Role of Forts, Dens and Bush Houses in Middle Childhood; David Sobel; Wayne State University Press

Foxes and Their Dens; Martha E. H. Rustad; Capstone Press

A Den, a Tree, a Nest Is Best; Katharine Kenah; School Specialty Publishing

The Den; Adam Stower; Bloomsbury Publishing

Tree Houses You Can Actually Build; David Stiles; Houghton Mifflin

Build Your Own Fantasy Treehouse; David Parfitt; David & Charles

Making Make-believe: Fun Props, Costumes and Creative Play Ideas; MaryAnn F. Kohl; Gryphon House

Come Home with Us; OXFAM; Child's Play

The Nest (Ecology Story Books); Chris Baines; Frances Lincoln

Wasp's Nest; Kate Scarborough; Hodder Wayland

Woodworking for Kids: 40 Things for Kids to Make; Kevin McGuire; Sterling Juvenile

Birdfeeders (Kids Can Do It); Renee Schwarz; Kids Can Press

Curriculum coverage grid overleaf

Potential NC KS1 Curriculum Coverage through the provocations suggested for ice.

Full version of KS1 PoS on pages 69-74
Photocopiable version on page 8

Literacy

	Lit 1 speak	Lit 2 listen	Lit 3 group	Lit 4 drama	Lit 5 word	Lit 6 spell	Lit 7 text1	Lit 8 text2	Lit 9 text3	Lit10 text4	Lit11 sentence	Lit12 presentation
Literacy	1.1	2.1	3.1	4.1	5.1	6.1	7.1	8.1	9.1	10.1	11.1	12.1
	1.2	2.2	3.2	4.2	5.2	6.2	7.2	8.2	9.2	10.2	11.2	12.2

Numeracy

	Num 1 U&A	Num 2 count	Num 3 number	Num 4 calculate	Num 5 shape	Num 6 measure	Num 7 data
Numeracy	1.1	2.1	3.1	4.1	5.1	6.1	7.1
	1.2	2.2	3.2	4.2	5.2	6.2	7.2

Science

	SC1 Enquiry			SC2 Life processes					SC3 Materials		SC4 Phys processes		
	Sc1.1	Sc1.2	Sc1.3	Sc2.1	Sc2.2	Sc2.3	Sc2.4	Sc2.5	Sc3.1	Sc3.2	Sc4.1	Sc4.2	Sc4.3
Science	1.1a	1.2a	1.3a	2.1a	2.2a	2.3a	2.4a	2.5a	3.1a	3.2a	4.1a	4.2a	4.3a
	1.1b	1.2b	1.3b	2.1b	2.2b	2.3b	2.4b	2.5b	3.1b	3.2b	4.1b	4.2b	4.3b
	1.1c	1.2c	1.3c	2.1c	2.2c	2.3c		2.5c	3.1c		4.1c	4.2c	4.3c
	1.1d				2.2d				3.1d				4.3d
					2.2e								
					2.2f								
					2.2g								

History

	H1 chronology	H2 events, people	H3 interpret	H4 enquire	H5 org & comm	H6 breadth
History	1a	2a	3a	4a	5a	6a
	1b	2b		4b		6b
						6c
						6d

Geography

	G1.1 & G1.2 enquiry		G2 places	G3 processes	G4 environment	G5 breadth
Geography	1.1a	1.2a	2a	3a	4a	5a
	1.1b	1.2b	2b	3b	4b	5b
	1.1c	1.2c	2c			5c
	1.1d	1.2d	2d			5d
			2e			

ICT

	ICT 1 finding out		ICT 2 ideas	ICT 3 reviewing	ICT 4 breadth
ICT	1.1a	1.2a	2a	3a	4a
	1.1b	1.2b	2b	3b	4b
	1.1c	1.2c	2c	3c	4c
		1.2d			

D&T

	D&T 1 developing	D&T 2 tool use	D&T 3 evaluating	D&T 4 materials	D&T 5 breadth
D&T	1a	2a	3a	4a	5a
	1b	2b	3b	4b	5b
	1c	2c			5c
	1d	2d			
	1e	2e			

Music

	M1 performing	M2 composing	M3 appraising	M4 listening	M5 breadth
Music	1a	2a	3a	4a	5a
	1b	2b	3b	4b	5b
	1c			4c	5c
					5d

PHSE & C

	PSHEC1 conf & resp	PSHEC2 citizenship	PSHEC3 health	PSHEC4 relationships
PHSE & C	1a	2a	3a	4a
	1b	2b	3b	4b
	1c	2c	3c	4c
	1d	2d	3d	4d
	1e	2e	3e	4e
		2f	3f	
		2g	3g	
		2h		

Art & Design

	A&D1 ideas	A&D2 making	A&D3 evaluating	A&D4 materials	A&D5 breadth
Art & Design	1a	2a	3a	4a	5a
	1b	2b	3b	4b	5b
		2c		4c	5c
					5d

PE

	PE1 devel skills	PE2 apply skills	PE3 evaluate	PE4 fitness	PE5 breadth
PE	1a	2a	3a	4a	5a dance
	1b	2b	3b	4b	5b games
		2c	3c		5c gym

Critical skills	Thinking Skills
problem solving	observing
decision making	classifying
critical thinking	prediction
creative thinking	making inferences
communication	problem solving
organisation	drawing conclusions
management	
leadership	

Weather and Seasons

Weather and Seasons

Previous experience in the Foundation Stage.

Projects on the weather and the seasons form a central part of the curriculum for science and knowledge of the world in the early years. Children may have had some of these experiences:

* looking at seasonal plants and flowers;
* watching what animals and birds do;
* watching and recording the weather;
* playing out of doors in different seasons and weathers;
* talking about clothing and footwear;
* cooking seasonal food;
* visiting parks and woodlands in different seasons;
* using their senses to explore different weather and times of year;
* seasonal songs, rhymes and poems.

Pause for thought

In the early stages of working with these materials it is crucial to continue to observe the children. Only by doing this can you set developmentally appropriate challenges and provocations. The ideas listed here are offered as suggestions; the most exciting challenges will arise from children's own interests and motivations, which will only become apparent as you spend time with them, watching and joining them in their play. As you do this, you will be moving between the three interconnecting roles of observer, co-player, extender described below, and will be able to decide what you need to do next to take the learning forward.

The responsive adult (see page 5)

In three interconnecting roles, the responsive adult will be:

* observing
* listening
* interpreting

observer

* modelling
* playing alongside
* offering suggestions
* responding sensitively
* initiating with care!

co-player

* discussing ideas
* sharing thinking
* modelling new skills
* asking open questions
* being an informed extender
* instigating ideas & thoughts
* supporting children as they make links in learning
* making possibilities evident
* introducing new ideas and resources
* offering challenges and provocations

extender

Offering Challenges and Provocations - some ideas:

? What season is it now? How do you know? use a camera to record some signs of the season.

? Make a weather chart for a week. decide on some symbols for each sort of weather and use these to record the weather every day. You can find the TV weather symbols on the BBC weather site www.bbc.co.uk/weather.

? Can you make a book with ideas for games to play in each of the four seasons. Get your friends to play the games and take photos of them to illustrate your book.

? Do you know which flowers bloom in each season? Could you make a chart to show this?

? Go outside and look at the sky. What can you see? Watch the sky for fifteen minutes. How does it change? make a list of all the things you saw happening in the sky as you watched.

? Can you invent a rain catcher using recycled materials? Draw your design, then make the rain catcher and leave it outside to catch the rain. How well does it work? Could you improve it?

? Start a bird watching diary for your class to use. Take turns to watch the birds every day and record what you all see. Use books and the internet to find out which birds visit your garden or school grounds.

? Birds will come if you make some bird feeders. Find out how to do this, and remember to feed the birds every day, even in the summer.

? Make a book about your favourite season. Paint a cover using colours that match the season.

Ready for more?

- Can you design a weather mobile that responds to wind, rain and sun? make your mobile and hang it up outside.

- Can you make a weather station? decide what you need to measure and collect.
Remember that you need to measure wind, rain, temperature, sunshine. How can you do this. Use the internet to help.

- Make a sundial in your garden or grounds. Look at www.bbc.co.uk/norfolk/kids or www.nmm.ac.uk and search 'sundial'. Both sites have instructions and templates to print out.

- Go outside and collect some natural materials - leaves, seeds, petals, twigs. Can you use these to make a seasonal collage? You could weave them into netting, or stick them on card or fabric. How could you protect your collage so you can hang it outside?

- Try this on a windy day. Go outside and see if you can measure how strong the wind is in different parts of the playground or school grounds. What can you use to measure the wind? You may need a friend to help. Record what you find out, using a camera.

- Find out how to press flowers. make a flower press and press some seasonal flowers to make greeting cards, gift tags or calendars. Always ask before picking flowers, even weeds belong to someone!

Materials, equipment, suppliers, websites, books and other references

Watching and recording the weather is a simple activity that really keeps children in touch with the natural world. You don't need an expensive weather chart or station just a routine for watching and a system for recording.

- Photos are a really good way of recording the weather and the seasons. Encourage the children to take photos from the same place every day or during each season. Then you can make slide shows or photo books.

- Make a habit of watching or listening to the weather forecast and checking whether what is forecast is what really happens.

- Hang up simple objects that will alert the children to the weather - CDs, streamers, windsocks, prayer flags, metal pans to catch the sound of water, windmills, sundials, an unbreakable mirror on the floor to reflect the sky.

Research and provide some shelters for extreme weather - bright sun, cold winds, showers. gazebos and tents are good ways of enabling children to be outside in all weathers.

Try **Google Images** 'seasons' or 'winter' 'spring' 'summer' 'autumn' 'sun' 'wind' 'rain' 'clouds' 'storms' 'hurricane' for some really good and colourful photos.

There are lots of internet sites for making a weather station, but some sites really need adult help - www.fi.edu/weather and www.bbc.co.uk/tyne/weather - for weather station instructions www.bbc.co.uk/weather/weatherwise/activities - for useful information for adults and children or go to fun.familyeducation.com/Children's-science-activities/weather and find the activity 'rain in a bag'.

Some books:

The Kid's Book of Weather Forecasting; Mark Breen; Williamson Publishing Company
Winter/Spring/Autumn/Summer; Nature Activities for Children; Irmgard Kutsch; Floris Books
Weather Detectives; Mark Eubank; Gibbs Smith
Crafts for Kids Who Are Learning about Weather; Kathy Ross; Millbrook Press
The Wind Blew; Pat Hutchins; Aladdin
What Makes the Wind?; Laurence Santrey; Troll Communications
How Weather Works; Michael Allaby; Readers Digest
Learning about Weather; Jo Ellen Moore; Evan-Moor Educational
Tell Me Why Rain Is Wet; Shirley Willis; Franklin Watts
Weather - Scienceworks; Rose/Graf; Evan-Moor Educational
Skip Through the Seasons; Stella Blackstone; Barefoot Books
Autumn/Spring/Summer/Winter (Go Facts: Seasons); Katy Pike; A & C Black
Autumn Activity Book; Clare Beaton; b small publishing
A Golden Leaf; The Story of Autumn; Rosie McCormick; Hodder Wayland
The Seasons (Poetry for Young People); John N. Serio; Sterling Publishing
Poems About Seasons; Andrew Fusek; Hodder Wayland

Curriculum coverage grid overleaf

Literacy

Lit 1 speak	Lit 2 listen	Lit 3 group	Lit 4 drama	Lit 5 word	Lit 6 spell	Lit 7 text1	Lit 8 text2	Lit 9 text3	Lit10 text4	Lit11 sentence	Lit12 presentation
1.1	2.1	3.1	4.1	5.1	6.1	7.1	8.1	9.1	10.1	11.1	12.1
1.2	2.2	3.2	4.2	5.2	6.2	7.2	8.2	9.2	10.2	11.2	12.2

Numeracy

Num 1 U&A	Num 2 count	Num 3 number	Num 4 calculate	Num 5 shape	Num 6 measure	Num 7 data
1.1	2.1	3.1	4.1	5.1	6.1	7.1
1.2	2.2	3.2	4.2	5.2	6.2	7.2

Full version of KS1 PoS on pages 69-74
Photocopiable version on page 8

Science

SC1 Enquiry			SC2 Life processes					SC3 Materials		SC4 Phys processes		
Sc1.1	Sc1.2	Sc1.3	Sc2.1	Sc2.2	Sc2.3	Sc2.4	Sc2.5	Sc3.1	Sc3.2	Sc4.1	Sc4.2	Sc4.3
1.1a	1.2a	1.3a	2.1a	2.2a	2.3a	2.4a	2.5a	3.1a	3.2a	4.1a	4.2a	4.3a
1.1b	1.2b	1.3b	2.1b	2.2b	2.3b	2.4b	2.5b	3.1b	3.2b	4.1b	4.2b	4.3b
1.1c	1.2c	1.3c	2.1c	2.2c	2.3c		2.5c	3.1c		4.1c	4.2c	4.3c
1.1d				2.2d				3.1d				4.3d
				2.2e								
				2.2f								
				2.2g								

ICT

ICT 1 finding out		ICT 2 ideas	ICT 3 reviewing	ICT 4 breadth
1.1a	1.2a	2a	3a	4a
1.1b	1.2b	2b	3b	4b
1.1c	1.2c	2c	3c	4c
	1.2d			

D&T

D&T 1 developing	D&T 2 tool use	D&T 3 evaluating	D&T 4 materials	D&T 5 breadth
1a	2a	3a	4a	5a
1b	2b	3b	4b	5b
1c	2c			5c
1d	2d			
1e	2e			

History

H1 chronology	H2 events, people	H3 interpret	H4 enquire	H5 org & comm	H6 breadth
1a	2a	3a	4a	5a	6a
1b	2b		4b		6b
					6c
					6d

Geography

G1.1 & G1.2 enquiry		G2 places	G3 processes	G4 environment	G5 breadth
1.1a	1.2a	2a	3a	4a	5a
1.1b	1.2b	2b	3b	4b	5b
1.1c	1.2c	2c			5c
1.1d	1.2d	2d			5d
		2e			

Music

M1 performing	M2 composing	M3 appraising	M4 listening	M5 breadth
1a	2a	3a	4a	5a
1b	2b	3b	4b	5b
1c			4c	5c
				5d

PHSE & C

PSHEC1 conf & resp	PSHEC2 citizenship	PSHEC3 health	PSHEC4 relationships
1a	2a	3a	4a
1b	2b	3b	4b
1c	2c	3c	4c
1d	2d	3d	4d
1e	2e	3e	4e
	2f	3f	
	2g	3g	
	2h		

Art & Design

A&D1 ideas	A&D2 making	A&D3 evaluating	A&D4 materials	A&D5 breadth
1a	2a	3a	4a	5a
1b	2b	3b	4b	5b
	2c		4c	5c
				5d

PE

PE1 devel skills	PE2 apply skills	PE3 evaluate	PE4 fitness	PE5 breadth
1a	2a	3a	4a	5a dance
1b	2b	3b	4b	5b games
	2c	3c		5c gym

Critical skills	Thinking Skills
problem solving	observing
decision making	classifying
critical thinking	prediction
creative thinking	making inferences
communication	problem solving
organisation	drawing conclusions
management	
leadership	

Petals, Leaves, Feathers and Stones

Petals, Leaves, Feathers and Stones

Previous experience in the Foundation Stage.
The use of natural materials in the Foundation Stage is widespread - in art, craft, construction, science and technology. Children should have had wide experience of using these materials both in free play and in adult supported tasks and activities such as:

* collecting and discussing natural materials in free play, and during walks and visits;
* making constructions and other creations from sticks, stones, leaves, shells and petals;
* using sticks, leaves and feathers to make hangings and collages;
* using sticks, stones etc to represent other objects - money, gifts, tickets, tokens - and to count and sort.

Pause for thought
In the early stages of working with these materials it is crucial to continue to observe the children. Only by doing this can you set developmentally appropriate challenges and provocations. The ideas listed here are offered as suggestions; the most exciting challenges will arise from children's own interests and motivations, which will only become apparent as you spend time with them, watching and joining them in their play. As you do this, you will be moving between the three interconnecting roles of observer, co-player, extender described below, and will be able to decide what you need to do next to take the learning forward.

The responsive adult (see page 5)

In three interconnecting roles, the responsive adult will be:

observer

* observing
* listening
* interpreting

co-player

* modelling
* playing alongside
* offering suggestions
* responding sensitively
* initiating with care!

extender

* discussing ideas
* sharing thinking
* modelling new skills
* asking open questions
* being an informed extender
* instigating ideas & thoughts
* supporting children as they make links in learning
* making possibilities evident
* introducing new ideas and resources
* offering challenges and provocations

Offering Challenges and Provocations - some ideas:

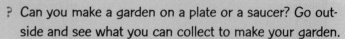

Collect a range of longer lasting natural objects that can be used for construction, sorting and creative play - sticks, sawn logs, bark, compost, stones, pebbles and shells, seasonal items such as conkers and nuts, hay and straw. Add some more ephemeral objects such as flowers, petals, feathers, leaves, grass, seaweed, moss etc.

? Can you make a garden on a plate or a saucer? Go outside and see what you can collect to make your garden.

? Try painting and writing with natural materials - feathers, sticks, moss, flowers - which are best for writing with, which are best for pictures?

? Go for a walk round your outdoor area or garden. Take a carrier bag with you and see how many natural objects you can find. When you have finished, sort your collection out and photograph it.

? Look carefully at your collection with a magnifying glass. What can you see? Record all the tiny things you find.

? Find 25 stones or pebbles. Set these out in a line from the biggest to the smallest. Take a photo or draw your line. Now reorganise the pebbles by weight. Draw or photograph the new line. Is it different? Now organise the pebbles by colour or texture.

? Find a crayon or coloured pencil. Go outside and see if you can find something that is exactly the same colour as your crayon or pencil. Now try with another colour.

? Find some leaves. Sort them into different shapes and sizes. How many different sorts of leaves are there? Look in books and see if you can find out what the different shapes are called.

? Collect some sticks, stones, leaves and other natural materials. get some wool or string and make a hanging with natural objects, by tying them onto a length of string. Find a place outside to display your hangings.

Ready for more?

- Use conkers, acorns, fir cones and other nuts or seeds to make sequences and repeating patterns.
- Can you find out about Rangoli Patterns? Look on Google images 'rangoli'. Use natural materials such as sand, pebbles, petals and leaves to make Rangoli patterns. There is an example on this page.
- Find some leaves or stones. Now can you mix paints that are exactly the same colours as your leaves and stones? Use your colours to make a painting of the leaves and stones and display them together.
- Work with four friends. Go outside and collect or dig up some stones. Wash the stones and each choose the one you like best. Do a pencil, charcoal or pastel drawing of your favourite stone and make an exhibition. See if other children can match the stones to the drawings.
- Look up 'Andy Goldsworthy' on Google images. Click on some of the images to find out how this artist uses flowers, stones and wood to make art works. Have a go your selves!
- In winter, go for a walk and collect dead seed heads, skeleton leaves, grasses and other natural objects of winter. Make a display. If you made a display of the natural objects of summer, would it look different?

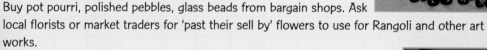

Materials, equipment suppliers, websites, books and other references

Suppliers; Try to collect some baskets or boxes of stones, leaves, nuts, feathers, cones and other natural objects - keep these fresh by removing the old ones and replacing with collections from walks, visits, holidays and so on.

Always encourage children to pick up natural materials for the collection, and ask them to bring a shell, pebble, cone, leaf or a piece of driftwood from their holidays and you'll soon have a collection!

The message about collecting natural objects should always be **"If it isn't fixed on, it is likely to be OK. If it is fixed on - ask!"**

Buy pot pourri, polished pebbles, glass beads from bargain shops. Ask local florists or market traders for 'past their sell by' flowers to use for Rangoli and other art works.

Provide small containers, string and netting, shallow trays, plastic plates for creations and gardens. Offer peat and sand as a base for art work.

Look up **'Rangoli'** on the internet and find out about this form of art, originally found on doorsteps. You can also download versions of rangoli patterns to use as bases for your creations with real petals, leaves, sand etc.

Try **Google Images**: 'natural art' 'art from nature' 'Andy Goldsworthy' 'natural collage' 'pebble art' 'painted stone' 'rangoli' 'petals' 'leaves'.

Some **books**:

Sharing Nature with Children; Joseph Cornell; Dawn Publications
Arts in the School Grounds; Brian Keaney; Learning Through Landscapes
Hands-on Nature; Jenepher Lingelbach; University Press of New England
Engaging Places; Commission for Architecture and the Built Environment (CABE)
Challenge of the Urban School Site; Learning through Landscapes
Nature's Playground; Fiona Danks; Frances Lincoln
Ecoart!; Lauri Carlson; Williamson Publishing

Remind children to wash their hands after working with materials from out of doors.

Potential NC KS1 Curriculum Coverage through the provocations suggested for petals, stones etc.

Full version of KS1 PoS on pages 69-74
Photocopiable version on page 8

Literacy	Lit 1 speak	Lit 2 listen	Lit 3 group	Lit 4 drama	Lit 5 word	Lit 6 spell	Lit 7 text1	Lit 8 text2	Lit 9 text3	Lit10 text4	Lit11 sentence	Lit12 presentation
	1.1	2.1	3.1	4.1	5.1	6.1	7.1	8.1	9.1	10.1	11.1	12.1
	1.2	2.2	3.2	4.2	5.2	6.2	7.2	8.2	9.2	10.2	11.2	12.2

Numeracy	Num 1 U&A	Num 2 count	Num 3 number	Num 4 calculate	Num 5 shape	Num 6 measure	Num 7 data
	1.1	2.1	3.1	4.1	5.1	6.1	7.1
	1.2	2.2	3.2	4.2	5.2	6.2	7.2

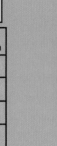

Science	SC1 Enquiry			SC2 Life processes					SC3 Materials		SC4 Phys processes		
	Sc1.1	Sc1.2	Sc1.3	Sc2.1	Sc2.2	Sc2.3	Sc2.4	Sc2.5	Sc3.1	Sc3.2	Sc4.1	Sc4.2	Sc4.3
	1.1a	1.2a	1.3a	2.1a	2.2a	2.3a	2.4a	2.5a	3.1a	3.2a	4.1a	4.2a	4.3a
	1.1b	1.2b	1.3b	2.1b	2.2b	2.3b	2.4b	2.5b	3.1b	3.2b	4.1b	4.2b	4.3b
	1.1c	1.2c	1.3c	2.1c	2.2c	2.3c		2.5c	3.1c		4.1c	4.2c	4.3c
	1.1d				2.2d				3.1d				4.3d
					2.2e								
					2.2f								
					2.2g								

ICT	ICT 1 finding out		ICT 2 ideas	ICT 3 reviewing	ICT 4 breadth
	1.1a	1.2a	2a	3a	4a
	1.1b	1.2b	2b	3b	4b
	1.1c	1.2c	2c	3c	4c
		1.2d			

D&T	D&T 1 developing	D&T 2 tool use	D&T 3 evaluating	D&T 4 materials	D&T 5 breadth
	1a	2a	3a	4a	5a
	1b	2b	3b	4b	5b
	1c	2c			5c
	1d	2d			
	1e	2e			

History	H1 chronology	H2 events, people	H3 interpret	H4 enquire	H5 org & comm	H6 breadth
	1a	2a	3a	4a	5a	6a
	1b	2b		4b		6b
						6c
						6d

Geography	G1.1 & G1.2 enquiry		G2 places	G3 processes	G4 environment	G5 breadth
	1.1a	1.2a	2a	3a	4a	5a
	1.1b	1.2b	2b	3b	4b	5b
	1.1c	1.2c	2c			5c
	1.1d	1.2d	2d			5d
			2e			

Music	M1 performing	M2 composing	M3 appraising	M4 listening	M5 breadth
	1a	2a	3a	4a	5a
	1b	2b	3b	4b	5b
	1c			4c	5c
					5d

PHSE & C	PSHEC1 conf & resp	PSHEC2 citizenship	PSHEC3 health	PSHEC4 relationships
	1a	2a	3a	4a
	1b	2b	3b	4b
	1c	2c	3c	4c
	1d	2d	3d	4d
	1e	2e	3e	4e
		2f	3f	
		2g	3g	
		2h		

Art& Design	A&D1 ideas	A&D2 making	A&D3 evaluating	A&D4 materials	A&D5 breadth
	1a	2a	3a	4a	5a
	1b	2b	3b	4b	5b
		2c		4c	5c
					5d

PE	PE1 devel skills	PE2 apply skills	PE3 evaluate	PE4 fitness	PE5 breadth
	1a	2a	3a	4a	5a dance
	1b	2b	3b	4b	5b games
		2c	3c		5c gym

Critical skills	Thinking Skills
problem solving	observing
decision making	classifying
critical thinking	prediction
creative thinking	making inferences
communication	problem solving
organisation	drawing conclusions
management	
leadership	

Bats, Balls and Beanbags

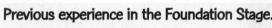
Bats, balls and beanbags

Previous experience in the Foundation Stage.

Throughout the Early Years Foundation Stage, children will have played with a range of different sized balls in both adult and child initiated activities. They will have:

* patted;
* bounced;
* kicked;
* rolled;
* thrown and caught balls.

They may have had less experience of bats, which require a far greater degree of co-ordination and control.

Pause for thought

In the early stages of working with these materials it is crucial to continue to observe the children. Only by doing this can you set developmentally appropriate challenges and provocations. The ideas listed here are offered as suggestions; the most exciting challenges will arise from children's own interests and motivations, which will only become apparent as you spend time with them, watching and joining them in their play. As you do this, you will be moving between the three interconnecting roles of observer, co-player, extender described below, and will be able to decide what you need to do next to take the learning forward.

The responsive adult (see page 5)

In three interconnecting roles, the responsive adult will be:

observer

* observing
* listening
* interpreting

co-player

* modelling
* playing alongside
* offering suggestions
* responding sensitively
* initiating with care!

extender

* discussing ideas
* sharing thinking
* modelling new skills
* asking open questions
* being an informed extender
* instigating ideas & thoughts
* supporting children as they make links in learning
* making possibilities evident
* introducing new ideas and resources
* offering challenges and provocations

Offering Challenges and Provocations - some ideas:

NOTE: In order for children to develop their skills further, there is plenty of scope for continued free play with bats and balls, where children can explore at their own pace, supported by sympathetic adults.

Some children in Year 1 may still find it difficult to catch a ball, so try using something that travels through the air at a slower pace, such as:

* a balloon
* a balloon wrapped in a headscarf
* a beanbag
* a 'koosh ball'.

? Make a collection of balls of different sizes. How many can you find? How can you measure which is biggest and which is smallest?

? Can you make up some new ball games, using your new collection of different balls?

? Can you invent some games by combining balls with other things such as:
* plastic buckets?
* playground chalk?
* plastic bottles, empty or filled with sand or water?
* guttering and drainpipes?
* wire coat hangers to make hoops in grass areas for balls to go through?

? Write some instructions for playing these games.

? Look in books and on the internet to find out how to play new ball games. Try some of them out.

? Invent some games for bats and balls. Can you make up:
* a target game?
* a game using numbers?
* a passing game?
* a team game?
* a 'tag' game?
* a parachute game?

Remember, all the games must use at least one ball and at least one bat. Play the games to check they really work!

Ready for more?

- Find out how balls were made in the past. Look on the Internet and in books. Ask your relatives and older people you know. Contact your local museum or sports club to see if they can tell you anything.
- Experiment with making a ball. What can you use? Recycled materials work well. You could try using:
  - elastic bands
  - newspaper
  - string
  - stuffed plastic bags
  - old CDs or postcards
  - tin cans or bottles.

  Look on Google Images 'making balls' for some help and ideas.
- Throw your ball against a wall or into the air. While it is in the air, clap you hands, then catch the ball again. Try again - can you clap twice, or three times? Can you clap your hands above your head, or behind your back before catching the ball again?
- Have a contest with your friends. Who can clap the most times after throwing the ball in the air, and before they catch it? Can they throw the ball, turn round, then catch it again?
- Record the results and then see if you can beat the record.
- Can you use more than one ball to juggle? Some people can juggle with three or four balls. Find out how to do it.

ascoeducational.co.uk

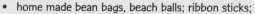
ascoeducational.co.uk

Materials, equipment suppliers, websites, books and other references

ascoeducational.co.uk

Suppliers and sources:

Outdoor PE equipment is easy to find and cheap in educational supply and consortium catalogues. If you want some different ideas, try ascoeducational.co.uk. You could also add:

- home made bean bags, beach balls; ribbon sticks;
- playground chalk, black or white boards and markers;
- trundle wheels;
- buckets;
- a parachute.

ascoeducational.co.uk

Use Google Images for pictures - some suggestions for words to search: 'playground games' 'Victorian playground games' 'skittles' or other games.

Google web for 'make your own skittles' or the name of any other game will give you instructions on making your own equipment and games. www.playgroundfun.org.uk is a site for children with a range of different games and tips for adults on using them in school. Or try www.llanddulas.conwy.sch.uk where you can find some good pictures and instructions for playing some of the best playground games.

ascoeducational.co.uk

Some books and stories:

Outdoor Fun and Games for Kids; 100+ Activities for 3-11s; Jane Kemp; Hamlyn

Outdoor Activities for Kids; 100+ Things to Do Outside; Clare Brad; Lorenz Books

Creating a Space to Grow; Gail Ryder-Richardson; David Fulton

Primary Playground Games; Cat Weatherill; Scholastic

The Little Book of Playground Games; Simon MacDonald and

The Little Book of Parachute Play; Clare Beswick; Featherstone Education

The Jump Rope Book; Elizabeth Loredo; Workman Publishing

ascoeducational.co.uk

EarthFriendly Outdoor Fun: Make Fabulous Games, Gardens, and Other Projects from Reusable Objects; George Pfiffner; Jossey Bass

Curriculum coverage grid overleaf

Full version of KS1 PoS on pages 69-74
Photocopiable version on page 8

Literacy

	Lit 1 speak	Lit 2 listen	Lit 3 group	Lit 4 drama	Lit 5 word	Lit 6 spell	Lit 7 text1	Lit 8 text2	Lit 9 text3	Lit10 text4	Lit11 sentence	Lit12 presentation
Literacy	1.1	2.1	3.1	4.1	5.1	6.1	7.1	8.1	9.1	10.1	11.1	12.1
	1.2	2.2	3.2	4.2	5.2	6.2	7.2	8.2	9.2	10.2	11.2	12.2

Numeracy

	Num 1 U&A	Num 2 count	Num 3 number	Num 4 calculate	Num 5 shape	Num 6 measure	Num 7 data
Numeracy	1.1	2.1	3.1	4.1	5.1	6.1	7.1
	1.2	2.2	3.2	4.2	5.2	6.2	7.2

Science

	SC1 Enquiry			SC2 Life processes					SC3 Materials		SC4 Phys processes		
	Sc1.1	Sc1.2	Sc1.3	Sc2.1	Sc2.2	Sc2.3	Sc2.4	Sc2.5	Sc3.1	Sc3.2	Sc4.1	Sc4.2	Sc4.3
Science	1.1a	1.2a	1.3a	2.1a	2.2a	2.3a	2.4a	2.5a	3.1a	3.2a	4.1a	4.2a	4.3a
	1.1b	1.2b	1.3b	2.1b	2.2b	2.3b	2.4b	2.5b	3.1b	3.2b	4.1b	4.2b	4.3b
	1.1c	1.2c	1.3c	2.1c	2.2c	2.3c		2.5c	3.1c		4.1c	4.2c	4.3c
	1.1d				2.2d				3.1d				4.3d
					2.2e								
					2.2f								
					2.2g								

ICT

	ICT 1 finding out		ICT 2 ideas	ICT 3 reviewing	ICT 4 breadth
ICT	1.1a	1.2a	2a	3a	4a
	1.1b	1.2b	2b	3b	4b
	1.1c	1.2c	2c	3c	4c
		1.2d			

ascoeducational.co.uk

D&T

	D&T 1 developing	D&T 2 tool use	D&T 3 evaluating	D&T 4 materials	D&T 5 breadth
D&T	1a	2a	3a	4a	5a
	1b	2b	3b	4b	5b
	1c	2c			5c
	1d	2d			
	1e	2e			

History

	H1 chronology	H2 events, people	H3 interpret	H4 enquire	H5 org & comm	H6 breadth
History	1a	2a	3a	4a	5a	6a
	1b	2b		4b		6b
						6c
						6d

Geography

	G1.1 & G1.2 enquiry		G2 places	G3 processes	G4 environment	G5 breadth
Geography	1.1a	1.2a	2a	3a	4a	5a
	1.1b	1.2b	2b	3b	4b	5b
	1.1c	1.2c	2c			5c
	1.1d	1.2d	2d			5d
			2e			

Music

	M1 performing	M2 composing	M3 appraising	M4 listening	M5 breadth
Music	1a	2a	3a	4a	5a
	1b	2b	3b	4b	5b
	1c			4c	5c
					5d

PSHE & C

	PSHEC1 conf & resp	PSHEC2 citizenship	PSHEC3 health	PSHEC4 relationships
PHSE & C	1a	2a	3a	4a
	1b	2b	3b	4b
	1c	2c	3c	4c
	1d	2d	3d	4d
	1e	2e	3e	4e
		2f	3f	
		2g	3g	
		2h		

Art & Design

	A&D1 ideas	A&D2 making	A&D3 evaluating	A&D4 materials	A&D5 breadth
Art & Design	1a	2a	3a	4a	5a
	1b	2b	3b	4b	5b
		2c		4c	5c
					5d

ascoeducational.co.uk

PE

	PE1 devel skills	PE2 apply skills	PE3 evaluate	PE4 fitness	PE5 breadth
PE	1a	2a	3a	4a	5a dance
	1b	2b	3b	4b	5b games
		2c	3c		5c gym

Critical skills	Thinking Skills
problem solving	observing
decision making	classifying
critical thinking	prediction
creative thinking	making inferences
communication	problem solving
organisation	drawing conclusions
management	
leadership	

Numbers

Numbers

Previous experience in the Foundation Stage.

Children may have already had experience of using numbers out of doors in:

* collecting and counting objects they see, find and are shown in the environment;
* recording scores for games;
* writing numbers with chalk or paint;
* singing and chanting counting and number songs and games such as 'What's the Time Mr Wolf?';
* playing counting games marked on the ground, or counting in ring games;
* playing games with natural objects;
* in pretend shopping, home play and other roles;
* counting seeds as they plant them, measuring the growth of plants.

Pause for thought

In the early stages of working with these materials it is crucial to continue to observe the children. Only by doing this can you set developmentally appropriate challenges and provocations. The ideas listed here are offered as suggestions; the most exciting challenges will arise from children's own interests and motivations, which will only become apparent as you spend time with them, watching and joining them in their play. As you do this, you will be moving between the three interconnecting roles of observer, co-player, extender described below, and will be able to decide what you need to do next to take the learning forward.

The responsive adult (see page 5)

In three interconnecting roles, the responsive adult will be:

observer

* observing
* listening
* interpreting

co-player

* modelling
* playing alongside
* offering suggestions
* responding sensitively
* initiating with care!

extender

* discussing ideas
* sharing thinking
* modelling new skills
* asking open questions
* being an informed extender
* instigating ideas & thoughts
* supporting children as they make links in learning
* making possibilities evident
* introducing new ideas and resources
* offering challenges and provocations

Offering Challenges and Provocations - some ideas:

Children should continue all the activities they have enjoyed in Reception, with added challenge of bigger numbers and more adventurous ideas. Children in key Stage 1 can work in pairs and groups to explore and invent games and use numbers.

? Find some playground chalk and draw some long, straight lines on the ground outside. Find out which line is longest by measuring and counting. Now draw some wiggly lines and find out which is the longest one of these.

? Do this with a friend or two. Find a stopwatch or timer and time yourselves doing these things:
  * running round the playground
  * scoring three goals with a football
  * hopping round in a big circle
  * touching every tree in the garden
  * finding something small and green
  Find a way to record your times.

? Find some bean bags and play a counting game outside. Write your scores on the ground with chalk.

? Get two buckets and some small balls (pingpong balls are good fun). Make up a counting game with the buckets and balls.

? Use a water tray or builder's tray and make a fishing games. Make the fish from waterproof recycled materials, write numbers on them with a waterproof marker, and use small strainers or nets to catch the fish.

? How many of these can you find or see in your garden in five minutes?
  * minibeasts - such as ants, snails and spiders;
  * birds - flying, perching, eating;
  * flowers - on weeds, bushes, trees or hedges as well as on garden plants;
  * vehicles - cars, bikes, aeroplanes, vans, buses, lorries.
  Record your findings in any way you choose.

Ready for more?

- Make a list of all the playground games you know. Now make a chart and find out which are the five most popular games in your class. Play these games, take photos and make a book with instructions.
- Find some skittles of small playground cones. Mark these with numbers and make up a game to play with them. Design a score sheet to use, then test the game with your friends.
- Make a target on the ground or the wall, number the target circles, and use bean bags or wet sponges to play a throwing game. Write your scores on a white board.
- Do a garden count. Plan the count first and make a recording chart. Include some of these in your count:
  - trees, bushes and plants;
  - places to sit;
  - habitats for animals, insects, birds;
  - risky or dangerous places.

  You could add photos or a plan to your results and make a display.
- Find a stopwatch or timer and challenge a group of friends to do some outdoor tasks against the clock. You decide what to ask them to do. Include all sorts of challenges, not just running. You could get them to search, dig, construct, work with sand or water, or make something.
- Make a set of giant dominoes, number bean bags or draughts and make an outdoor playing board with chalk or paint.

Materials, equipment suppliers, websites, books and other references

Resources:

Counting and number activities mostly involve taking resources from inside into the garden. Here are some ways you could do this:

- put some chalk, white boards and other counting items in a basket or bag for outdoor activities;
- have a small trolley or tiered vegetable basket for equipment;
- provide bags, small backpacks, belts with clips etc for writing implements, games kit such as balls and other small equipment.

Google images: 'children's games' 'parachute' 'number games' 'counting games' 'giant dominoes' 'giant chess' 'outdoor games' and **Google web search** for information on large size, outdoor games:

www.bbc.co.uk/parenting/play_and_do/primary_outdoor for outdoor games for 7-11 year olds
www.funandgames.org and click through to games for hundreds of different games to play
www.greatgardengames.com a site that sells big size garden games - good for ideas
www.gameskidsplay.net games compendium site; www.woodlands-junior.kent.sch.uk a school site with playground games including a giant version of Connect
www.find-me-a-gift.co.uk has a great photo of a giant Ludo set you could use as an idea and //sunshinebits.com has other giant versions of games
www.leics.gov.uk/foundation_maths_outside.doc - a download of ideas for the Foundation Stage, but still useful for KS1
www.kidscape.org.uk - has a leaflet on safer, nicer playtimes.

Books and Publications:

Primary Playground Games; Cat Weatherill; Scholastic
Get Out! Outdoor Activities Kids Can Enjoy Anywhere; Hallie Warshaw; Sterling Juvenile, US
The Little Book of Playground Games; Simon MacDonald; Featherstone Education
Juggling; Clive Gifford; Usborne
Making Waves: Exciting Parachute Games; Helen Sonnet; LDA
Great Big Book of Children's Games: 450+ Indoor & Outdoor Games for Kids; Derba Wise; McGraw Hill
The Outrageous Outdoor Games Book: 133 Group Projects, Games, and Activities; Bob Gregson; Fearon
Number Games; Rose Griffiths; A&C Black (good ideas for 'upsizing')
Go Figure!: Prizewinning book about numbers; Johnny Ball; DK

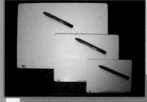

Curriculum coverage grid overleaf

Potential NC KS1 Curriculum Coverage through the provocations suggested for Numbers.

Literacy

	Lit 1 speak	Lit 2 listen	Lit 3 group	Lit 4 drama	Lit 5 word	Lit 6 spell	Lit 7 text1	Lit 8 text2	Lit 9 text3	Lit10 text4	Lit11 sentence	Lit12 presentation
Literacy	1.1	2.1	3.1	4.1	5.1	6.1	7.1	8.1	9.1	10.1	11.1	12.1
	1.2	2.2	3.2	4.2	5.2	6.2	7.2	8.2	9.2	10.2	11.2	12.2

Numeracy

	Num 1 U&A	Num 2 count	Num 3 number	Num 4 calculate	Num 5 shape	Num 6 measure	Num 7 data
Numeracy	1.1	2.1	3.1	4.1	5.1	6.1	7.1
	1.2	2.2	3.2	4.2	5.2	6.2	7.2

Science

	SC1 Enquiry			SC2 Life processes					SC3 Materials		SC4 Phys processes		
	Sc1.1	Sc1.2	Sc1.3	Sc2.1	Sc2.2	Sc2.3	Sc2.4	Sc2.5	Sc3.1	Sc3.2	Sc4.1	Sc4.2	Sc4.3
Science	1.1a	1.2a	1.3a	2.1a	2.2a	2.3a	2.4a	2.5a	3.1a	3.2a	4.1a	4.2a	4.3a
	1.1b	1.2b	1.3b	2.1b	2.2b	2.3b	2.4b	2.5b	3.1b	3.2b	4.1b	4.2b	4.3b
	1.1c	1.2c	1.3c	2.1c	2.2c	2.3c		2.5c	3.1c		4.1c	4.2c	4.3c
	1.1d				2.2d				3.1d				4.3d
					2.2e								
					2.2f								
					2.2g								

ICT

	ICT 1 finding out		ICT 2 ideas	ICT 3 reviewing	ICT 4 breadth
ICT	1.1a	1.2a	2a	3a	4a
	1.1b	1.2b	2b	3b	4b
	1.1c	1.2c	2c	3c	4c
		1.2d			

Full version of KS1 PoS on pages 69-74

Photocopiable version on page 8

D&T

	D&T 1 developing	D&T 2 tool use	D&T 3 evaluating	D&T 4 materials	D&T 5 breadth
D&T	1a	2a	3a	4a	5a
	1b	2b	3b	4b	5b
	1c	2c			5c
	1d	2d			
	1e	2e			

History

	H1 chronology	H2 events, people	H3 interpret	H4 enquire	H5 org & comm	H6 breadth
History	1a	2a	3a	4a	5a	6a
	1b	2b		4b		6b
						6c
						6d

Geography

	G1.1 & G1.2 enquiry		G2 places	G3 processes	G4 environment	G5 breadth
Geography	1.1a	1.2a	2a	3a	4a	5a
	1.1b	1.2b	2b	3b	4b	5b
	1.1c	1.2c	2c			5c
	1.1d	1.2d	2d			5d
			2e			

Music

	M1 performing	M2 composing	M3 appraising	M4 listening	M5 breadth
Music	1a	2a	3a	4a	5a
	1b	2b	3b	4b	5b
	1c			4c	5c
					5d

PSHE & C

	PSHEC1 conf & resp	PSHEC2 citizenship	PSHEC3 health	PSHEC4 relationships
PHSE & C	1a	2a	3a	4a
	1b	2b	3b	4b
	1c	2c	3c	4c
	1d	2d	3d	4d
	1e	2e	3e	4e
		2f	3f	
		2g	3g	
		2h		

Art & Design

	A&D1 ideas	A&D2 making	A&D3 evaluating	A&D4 materials	A&D5 breadth
Art & Design	1a	2a	3a	4a	5a
	1b	2b	3b	4b	5b
		2c		4c	5c
					5d

PE

	PE1 devel skills	PE2 apply skills	PE3 evaluate	PE4 fitness	PE5 breadth
PE	1a	2a	3a	4a	5a dance
	1b	2b	3b	4b	5b games
		2c	3c		5c gym

Critical skills	Thinking Skills
problem solving	observing
decision making	classifying
critical thinking	prediction
creative thinking	making inferences
communication	problem solving
organisation	drawing conclusions
management	
leadership	

Stories

Stories

Previous experience in the Foundation Stage.

There will be very few children who will not, at some time in the Early Years foundation Stage, have role-played 'We're Going on a Bear Hunt' outside. They may also have:

*   built houses for the Three Pigs;
*   made a beanstalk for Jack to climb;
*   played out Red Riding Hood's journey to Grandmother's house;
*   been the Three Bears, walking through the forest;
*   planned a trip to the Moon like the little bear in 'Whatever Next?';
*   been transformed into a Superhero story.

The challenge for KS1 teachers is to:

*   support children in expanding the challenge and complexity of their role play stories;
*   identify new stories for telling out of doors.

Pause for thought

In the early stages of working with these materials it is crucial to continue to observe the children. Only by doing this can you set developmentally appropriate challenges and provocations. The ideas listed here are offered as suggestions; the most exciting challenges will arise from children's own interests and motivations, which will only become apparent as you spend time with them, watching and joining them in their play. As you do this, you will be moving between the three interconnecting roles of observer, co-player, extender described below, and will be able to decide what you need to do next to take the learning forward.

The responsive adult (see page 5)

In three interconnecting roles, the responsive adult will be:

*   observing
*   listening
*   interpreting

observer

*   modelling
*   playing alongside
*   offering suggestions
*   responding sensitively
*   initiating with care!

co-player

*   discussing ideas
*   sharing thinking
*   modelling new skills
*   asking open questions
*   being an informed extender
*   instigating ideas & thoughts
*   supporting children as they make links in learning
*   making possibilities evident
*   introducing new ideas and resources
*   offering challenges and provocations

extender

Offering Challenges and Provocations - some ideas:

Encourage children to innovate and invent new versions of well known stories - for example:

?   Can you invent a new 'Bear Hunt' story - about a Lion Hunt, a Dragon Hunt, a Dinosaur Hunt, a Butterfly Hunt?

?   Someone else is in the Three Bears' House. Who might it be? What will happen next?

?   The Superheroes are planning a concert for the children in the hospital. What happens when they all show off their powers?

?   Can you make some props and costumes for your story? Use recycled materials and see what you can do.

?   Make some scenery for your story from shower curtains and big boxes.

?   Now photograph or video your story and make a computer presentation or a photo story book. Or you could laminate the photos and make them into an outdoor wall story mounted on a wall.

?   Create a performance area where you can act out your story with or without an audience.

?   Plan and build an outside den or area specially for stories. How many people can fit in your story space?

?   Design and build some spaces for stories outside, where you and your friends can go to read or write stories out of doors.

*   How will you make it comfortable?
*   How will you keep it warm and dry?
*   Who will choose and look after the books?
*   What will you provide for children who want to write or draw their own stories?

Ready for more?

- Can you make a collection of stories about pirates? Now can you make a place outside where you can play these stories? Can you make a boat?
- Can you make an outside listening area where children can go to listen to stories on CD or tape?
- Prop boxes help you to tell stories. Can you make a 'prop box' for one of your favourite stories, such as 'The Bear Hunt', 'Cinderella' or 'Finding Nemo'?
- Have a 'Story of the week'. Make an out-door prop box for the story.
- Find some stories that you can tell in a Builder's Tray or a big seed tray of compost, using small world people and animals. Photograph or film your stories and write your own story.
- Look for some stories about eggs. Do some nest building outside as you retell the story.
- Can you find stories about monsters, or robots, or scarecrows, or castles. Design scenery for retelling them out of doors.
- Recreate some stories about growing things and nature, and recreate these out of doors in trays and boxes.
- Find a way of making an island or a forest outside. Use this as the basis for telling stories.
- Work in groups to produce a concert for outdoor performance. Choose a theme such as Traditional Stories, Fantasy, Animal Stories, Adventure Islands.

Materials, equipment suppliers, websites, books and other references

The Bear Hunt

Some ideas for resources and equipment:

Drama outdoors needs inspiration, but this doesn't need to be complicated or directive. Try:

- a basket of fabrics (drapes and lengths of material) with pegs and other fastenings, wigs, hats, belts and other props;
- a backpack of story based materials - the children could collect these, or suggest items to add, stories to include etc;
- use puppets and soft toys to inspire story telling outside;
- set up story situations in pop-up tents, shelters, sheds and dens;
- offer small world animals and people for story making outside.

www.literacytrust.org.uk or www.standards.dfes.gov.uk/parentalinvolvement/pics/pics_storysacks for information on story sacks

www.storysack.com - is Neil Griffiths' site for his ready made story sacks for the primary age range

www.kidsonthenet.org.uk - a creative writing site for children

www.oakthorpe.enfield.sch.uk/tour - a school with an outdoor stage

www.playforce.co.uk or www.cookson-mcnally.co.uk/playspaces - both companies supply performance areas for schools, you could look here for ideas.

Google images: 'outdoor performance area' 'pop up tent' 'kids drama'.

Books and Other Publications:

101 Drama Games for Children, and **101 More Drama Games for Children**; Paul Rooyackers; Hunter House

Children Engaging with Drama; a downloadable version of the National Theatre report on their work with primary schools (website-archive2.nt-online.org)

How to Write a Play; Cyntha Rothman; Harcourt

Break a Leg! The Kids' Guide to Acting and Stagecraft; Lise Friedman; Workman Publishing

Making Make-believe: Fun Props, Costumes and Creative Play Ideas; MaryAnn F. Kohl; Gryphon House

and of course, any story, TV programme, topic or theme, or real-life incident that the children enjoy exploring can be turned into a short play, dance or drama session.

Curriculum coverage grid overleaf

Potential NC KS1 Curriculum Coverage through the provocations suggested for on the surface.

Full version of KS1 PoS on pages 69-74
Photocopiable version on page 8

Literacy	Lit 1 speak	Lit 2 listen	Lit 3 group	Lit 4 drama	Lit 5 word	Lit 6 spell	Lit 7 text1	Lit 8 text2	Lit 9 text3	Lit10 text4	Lit11 sentence	Lit12 presentation
	1.1	2.1	3.1	4.1	5.1	6.1	7.1	8.1	9.1	10.1	11.1	12.1
	1.2	2.2	3.2	4.2	5.2	6.2	7.2	8.2	9.2	10.2	11.2	12.2

Numeracy	Num 1 U&A	Num 2 count	Num 3 number	Num 4 calculate	Num 5 shape	Num 6 measure	Num 7 data
	1.1	2.1	3.1	4.1	5.1	6.1	7.1
	1.2	2.2	3.2	4.2	5.2	6.2	7.2

Science	SC1 Enquiry			SC2 Life processes					SC3 Materials		SC4 Phys processes		
	Sc1.1	Sc1.2	Sc1.3	Sc2.1	Sc2.2	Sc2.3	Sc2.4	Sc2.5	Sc3.1	Sc3.2	Sc4.1	Sc4.2	Sc4.3
	1.1a	1.2a	1.3a	2.1a	2.2a	2.3a	2.4a	2.5a	3.1a	3.2a	4.1a	4.2a	4.3a
	1.1b	1.2b	1.3b	2.1b	2.2b	2.3b	2.4b	2.5b	3.1b	3.2b	4.1b	4.2b	4.3b
	1.1c	1.2c	1.3c	2.1c	2.2c	2.3c		2.5c	3.1c		4.1c	4.2c	4.3c
	1.1d				2.2d				3.1d				4.3d
					2.2e								
					2.2f								
					2.2g								

ICT	ICT 1 finding out		ICT 2 ideas	ICT 3 reviewing	ICT 4 breadth
	1.1a	1.2a	2a	3a	4a
	1.1b	1.2b	2b	3b	4b
	1.1c	1.2c	2c	3c	4c
		1.2d			

D&T	D&T 1 developing	D&T 2 tool use	D&T 3 evaluating	D&T 4 materials	D&T 5 breadth
	1a	2a	3a	4a	5a
	1b	2b	3b	4b	5b
	1c	2c			5c
	1d	2d			
	1e	2e			

History	H1 chronology	H2 events, people	H3 interpret	H4 enquire	H5 org & comm	H6 breadth
	1a	2a	3a	4a	5a	6a
	1b	2b		4b		6b
						6c
						6d

Geography	G1.1 & G1.2 enquiry		G2 places	G3 processes	G4 environment	G5 breadth
	1.1a	1.2a	2a	3a	4a	5a
	1.1b	1.2b	2b	3b	4b	5b
	1.1c	1.2c	2c			5c
	1.1d	1.2d	2d			5d
			2e			

Music	M1 performing	M2 composing	M3 appraising	M4 listening	M5 breadth
	1a	2a	3a	4a	5a
	1b	2b	3b	4b	5b
	1c			4c	5c
					5d

PHSE & C	PSHEC1 conf & resp	PSHEC2 citizenship	PSHEC3 health	PSHEC4 relationships
	1a	2a	3a	4a
	1b	2b	3b	4b
	1c	2c	3c	4c
	1d	2d	3d	4d
	1e	2e	3e	4e
		2f	3f	
		2g	3g	
		2h		

Art & Design	A&D1 ideas	A&D2 making	A&D3 evaluating	A&D4 materials	A&D5 breadth
	1a	2a	3a	4a	5a
	1b	2b	3b	4b	5b
		2c		4c	5c
					5d

PE	PE1 devel skills	PE2 apply skills	PE3 evaluate	PE4 fitness	PE5 breadth
	1a	2a	3a	4a	5a dance
	1b	2b	3b	4b	5b games
		2c	3c		5c gym

Critical skills	Thinking Skills
problem solving	observing
decision making	classifying
critical thinking	prediction
creative thinking	making inferences
communication	problem solving
organisation	drawing conclusions
management	
leadership	

Games

Games

Previous experience in the Foundation Stage.
Children's experiences in playing collaborative games will vary considerably, but most will have some experience of playing:

* circle time games;
* chanting games such as 'In and Out the Dusty Bluebells', 'What's the Time Mr Wolf?' 'The Farmer's in his Den';
* throwing and catching games;
* target games;
* simple board games.

Pause for thought
In the early stages of working with these materials it is crucial to continue to observe the children. Only by doing this can you set developmentally appropriate challenges and provocations. The ideas listed here are offered as suggestions; the most exciting challenges will arise from children's own interests and motivations, which will only become apparent as you spend time with them, watching and joining them in their play. As you do this, you will be moving between the three interconnecting roles of observer, co-player, extender described below, and will be able to decide what you need to do next to take the learning forward.

The responsive adult (see page 5)

In three interconnecting roles, the responsive adult will be:

* observing
* listening
* interpreting

observer

* modelling
* playing alongside
* offering suggestions
* responding sensitively
* initiating with care!

co-player

* discussing ideas
* sharing thinking
* modelling new skills
* asking open questions
* being an informed extender
* instigating ideas & thoughts
* supporting children as they make links in learning
* making possibilities evident
* introducing new ideas and resources
* offering challenges and provocations

extender

Offering Challenges and Provocations - some ideas:

In order to get the most out of games, children first need to build up a wide repertoire of different sorts of games. Once they have done this, they can innovate and make up new versions, using their creativity to invent and expand on their knowledge.

? Can you invent your own version of 'Snakes and Ladders' by painting or chalking the board on the ground?

? Find a beanbag and a piece of chalk. How many games can you invent, using this equipment?

? Find a wall, a piece of chalk and a ball. Can you invent a target game?

? Can you make a collection of games that can be played outside. Put them in a book. How can you make it easy to find the games in the book?

? Ask your parents and other family members to tell you about games they know. Add these to your book.

? Could you publish your book of games on the school website so other children can play them? You may need some help with this!

? Could you print your book and sell it to other schools?

? Here are some different sorts of games you could include:

* games with trails
* treasure hunts
* games with bats and balls
* games with beanbags
* games with hoops
* games with skittles
* games with chalk
* large board games
* hopping, skipping and jumping games.

Ready for more?

- Find out about games from other cultures and countries. Try some of these games out.
- Interview some older people in the community or your grandparents. Find out what games they played when they were young. Try some of these.
- Can you make your own bats and balls from recycled materials? Find out how to make an elastic band ball (try Google).
- Find some empty plastic bottles. Fill them with water and use them to make your own skittles or a bowling alley.
- Make a game that is just about:
  - running
  - walking backwards with something on your head
  - lying down
  - finding things outside
  - some stones
  - different sorts of jumping.
- Make an obstacle race game. You can use some of these:
  - hoops
  - balls
  - dressing up clothes
  - beanbags
  - water
  - spoons.
- Invent some new games to be played in teams.
- Find out how to play Hopscotch.
- Invent a chanting game using names.

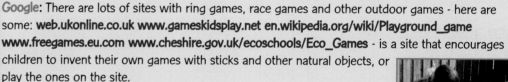

Materials, equipment suppliers, websites, books and other references

Some ideas for resources and equipment:

Educational suppliers and consortium groups have a huge range of equipment for game playing, but you could expand children's imaginative work in games by adding:

- plastic containers of all sorts;
- chalk and other mark makers;
- planks, tyres, fabrics and cable reels;
- boxes, bags and baskets;
- recycled materials to make their own bats, balls, containers;
- old clothes, scarves, hats etc for dressing up games and relay races;
- jugs, bottles, plastic plates, chopsticks, to use with sand, water, stones etc.

It's important to give children plenty of time to work on their invented games, and to find some way of keeping track of their early efforts by photos or simple clipboard notes.

Google: There are lots of sites with ring games, race games and other outdoor games - here are some: web.ukonline.co.uk www.gameskidsplay.net en.wikipedia.org/wiki/Playground_game www.freegames.eu.com www.cheshire.gov.uk/ecoschools/Eco_Games - is a site that encourages children to invent their own games with sticks and other natural objects, or play the ones on the site.

Books and Publications:

EarthFriendly Toys: Make Toys and Games from Reusable Objects (Earth-Friendly); George Pfiffner; Jossey Bass

Curriculum coverage grid overleaf

Potential NC KS1 Curriculum Coverage through the provocations suggested for games.

Full version of KS1 PoS on pages 69-74
Photocopiable version on page 8

Literacy

Lit 1 speak	Lit 2 listen	Lit 3 group	Lit 4 drama	Lit 5 word	Lit 6 spell	Lit 7 text1	Lit 8 text2	Lit 9 text3	Lit10 text4	Lit11 sentence	Lit12 presentation
1.1	2.1	3.1	4.1	5.1	6.1	7.1	8.1	9.1	10.1	11.1	12.1
1.2	2.2	3.2	4.2	5.2	6.2	7.2	8.2	9.2	10.2	11.2	12.2

Numeracy

Num 1 U&A	Num 2 count	Num 3 number	Num 4 calculate	Num 5 shape	Num 6 measure	Num 7 data
1.1	2.1	3.1	4.1	5.1	6.1	7.1
1.2	2.2	3.2	4.2	5.2	6.2	7.2

Science

SC1 Enquiry			SC2 Life processes					SC3 Materials		SC4 Phys processes		
Sc1.1	Sc1.2	Sc1.3	Sc2.1	Sc2.2	Sc2.3	Sc2.4	Sc2.5	Sc3.1	Sc3.2	Sc4.1	Sc4.2	Sc4.3
1.1a	1.2a	1.3a	2.1a	2.2a	2.3a	2.4a	2.5a	3.1a	3.2a	4.1a	4.2a	4.3a
1.1b	1.2b	1.3b	2.1b	2.2b	2.3b	2.4b	2.5b	3.1b	3.2b	4.1b	4.2b	4.3b
1.1c	1.2c	1.3c	2.1c	2.2c	2.3c		2.5c	3.1c		4.1c	4.2c	4.3c
1.1d				2.2d				3.1d				4.3d
				2.2e								
				2.2f								
				2.2g								

ICT

ICT 1 finding out		ICT 2 ideas	ICT 3 reviewing	ICT 4 breadth
1.1a	1.2a	2a	3a	4a
1.1b	1.2b	2b	3b	4b
1.1c	1.2c	2c	3c	4c
	1.2d			

History

H1 chronology	H2 events, people	H3 interpret	H4 enquire	H5 org & comm	H6 breadth
1a	2a	3a	4a	5a	6a
1b	2b		4b		6b
					6c
					6d

Geography

G1.1 & G1.2 enquiry		G2 places	G3 processes	G4 environment	G5 breadth
1.1a	1.2a	2a	3a	4a	5a
1.1b	1.2b	2b	3b	4b	5b
1.1c	1.2c	2c			5c
1.1d	1.2d	2d			5d
		2e			

D&T

D&T 1 developing	D&T 2 tool use	D&T 3 evaluating	D&T 4 materials	D&T 5 breadth
1a	2a	3a	4a	5a
1b	2b	3b	4b	5b
1c	2c			5c
1d	2d			
1e	2e			

Music

M1 performing	M2 composing	M3 appraising	M4 listening	M5 breadth
1a	2a	3a	4a	5a
1b	2b	3b	4b	5b
1c			4c	5c
				5d

PHSE & C

PSHEC1 conf & resp	PSHEC2 citizenship	PSHEC3 health	PSHEC4 relationships
1a	2a	3a	4a
1b	2b	3b	4b
1c	2c	3c	4c
1d	2d	3d	4d
1e	2e	3e	4e
	2f	3f	
	2g	3g	
	2h		

Art & Design

A&D1 ideas	A&D2 making	A&D3 evaluating	A&D4 materials	A&D5 breadth
1a	2a	3a	4a	5a
1b	2b	3b	4b	5b
	2c		4c	5c
				5d

PE

PE1 devel skills	PE2 apply skills	PE3 evaluate	PE4 fitness	PE5 breadth
1a	2a	3a	4a	5a dance
1b	2b	3b	4b	5b games
	2c	3c		5c gym

Critical skills	Thinking Skills
problem solving	observing
decision making	classifying
critical thinking	prediction
creative thinking	making inferences
communication	problem solving
organisation	drawing conclusions
management	
leadership	

The following pages contain the detail for the curriculum key which appears at the end of each section of the book. The appendix consists of the following:

1. Short-hand versions of the QCA/DfES Programme of Study for Key Stage 1 in:

> Science
> Information & Communication Technology
> Design and Technology
> History
> Geography
> Music
> Art and Design
> Physical Education

2. The suggested programme of study for Personal, Social and Health Education and Citizenship (PSHE & C)

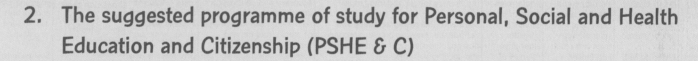

3. The elements of the guidance for learning and teaching of Literacy and Numeracy in Years 1 and 2 (from the Primary Framework for literacy and mathematics; DfES/SureStart; Sept 2006; Ref: 02011-2006BOK-EN)

Literacy 1 speaking	Literacy 2 listening & responding	Literacy 3 group discussion & interaction	Literacy 4 drama	Literacy 5 word recognition, coding & decoding	Literacy 6 word structure & spelling	Literacy 7 understanding & interpreting texts	Literacy 8 engaging & responding to text	Literacy 9 creating and shaping texts	Literacy 10 text structure & organisation	Literacy 11 sentence structure & punctuation	Literacy 12 presentation
Year 1 Tell stories and describe incidents from their own experience in an audible voice Retell stories, ordering events using story language Interpret a text by reading aloud with some variety in pace and emphasis **Experiment with & build new stores of words** to communicate in different contexts	**Year 1** Listen with sustained concentration, building new stores of words in different contexts Listen to and follow instructions accurately, asking for help and clarification if necessary Listen to tapes or video and express views about how a story or information has been presented	**Year 1** Take turns to speak, listen to others' suggestions and talk about what they are going to do Ask and answer questions, make relevant contributions, offer suggestions and take turns **Explain their views to others** in a small group, decide how to report the group's views to the class	**Year 1** Explore familiar themes and characters through improvisation and role-play Act out their own and well-known stories, using voices for characters Discuss why they like a performance	**Year 1** **Recognise & use alternative ways of pronouncing the graphemes already taught,** for example, that the grapheme 'g' is pronounced differently in 'get' and 'gem'; the grapheme 'ow' is pronounced differently in 'how' & 'show' **Recognise and use alternative ways of spelling the phonemes already taught,** for example 'ae' ' can be spelt with 'ai', 'ay' or 'a-e'; begin to know which words contain which spelling alternatives **Identify the constituent parts of two-syllable and three-syllable words** to support the application of phonic knowledge and skills Recognise automatically an increasing number of familiar high frequency words **Apply phonic knowledge & skills** as the prime approach to reading & spelling unfamiliar words that are not completely decodable **Read more challenging texts** which can be decoded using their acquired phonic knowledge & skills; automatic recognition of high frequency words Read and spell phonically decodable two-syllable and three-syllable words	**Year 1** Spell new words using phonics as the prime approach Segment sounds into their constituent phonemes in order to spell them correctly Children **move from spelling simple CVC words to longer words** that include common diagraphs & adjacent consonants such as 'brush', 'crunch' **Recognise & use alternative ways of spelling the graphemes already taught,** for example that the /ae/ sound can be spelt with 'ai', 'ay' or 'a-e'; that the /ee/ sound can also be spelt as 'ea' and 'e'; & begin to know which words contain which spelling alternatives **Use knowledge of common inflections in spelling,** such as plurals, -ly, -er **Read & spell phonically decodable 2- & 3 syllable words**	**Year 1** **Identify the main events and characters in stories,** and find specific information in simple texts **Use syntax and context when reading for meaning** **Make predictions** showing an understanding of ideas, events and characters **Recognise the main elements that shape different texts** **Explore the effect of patterns of language &** repeated words & phrases	**Year 1** Select books for personal reading and give reasons for choices **Visualise and comment on events, characters and ideas,** making imaginative links to their own experiences **Distinguish fiction and non-fiction texts** and the different purposes for reading them	**Year 1** **Independently choose what to write about,** plan and follow it through **Use key features of narrative in their own writing** Convey information and ideas in simple non-narrative forms **Find and use new and interesting words and phrases,** including story language **Create short simple texts on paper and on screen** that combine words with images (and sounds)	**Year 1** Write chronological and non-chronological texts using simple structures **Group written sentences together in chunks** of meaning or subject	**Year 1** Compose and write simple sentences independently to communicate meaning Use capital letters and full stops when punctuating simple sentences	**Year 1** Write most letters, correctly formed and orientated, using a comfortable and efficient pencil grip Write with spaces between words accurately Use the space bar and keyboard to type their name & simple texts
Year 2 Speak with clarity and use appropriate intonation when reading and reciting texts **Tell real and imagined stories** using the conventions of familiar story language **Explain ideas and processes** using imaginative and adventurous vocabulary and non-verbal gestures to support communication	**Year 2** Listen to others in class, ask relevant questions and follow instructions Listen to talk by an adult, remember some specific points and identify what they have learned **Respond to presentations** by describing characters, repeating some highlight and commenting constructively	**Year 2** Ensure that everyone contributes, allocate tasks, and consider alternatives and reach agreement **Work effectively in groups** by ensuring that each group member takes a turn challenging, supporting and moving on Listen to each other's views and preferences, agree the next steps to take and identify contributions by each group member	**Year 2** Adopt appropriate roles in small or large groups and consider alternative courses of action Present part of traditional stories, their own stories or work drawn from different parts of the curriculum for members of their own class **Consider how mood and atmosphere are created** in live or recorded performance	**Year 2** Read independently and with increasing fluency longer and less familiar texts Spell with increasing accuracy and confidence, drawing on word recognition and knowledge of word structure, and spelling patterns Know how to tackle unfamiliar words that are not completely decodable **Read and spell less common alternative graphemes including trigraphs** Read high and medium frequency words independently and automatically	**Year 2** Spell with increasing accuracy and confidence, drawing on word recognition and knowledge of word structure, and spelling patterns including common inflections and use of double letters Read and spell less common alternative graphemes including trigraphs **Understanding and interpreting texts**	**Year 2** Draw together ideas & information from across a whole text, using simple signposts in the text **Give reasons why things happen or characters change** **Explain organisational features of texts,** including alphabetical order, layout, diagrams etc **Use syntax & context** to build their store of vocabulary when reading **Explore how particular words are used,** including words & expressions with similar meanings	**Year 2** Read whole books on their own, choosing and justifying selections Engage with books through exploring and enacting interpretations **Explain their reactions to texts,** commenting on important aspects	**Year 2** Draw on knowledge and experience of texts in deciding and planning what & how to write **Sustain form in narrative,** including use of person & time Maintain consistency in non-narrative, including purpose & tense Make adventurous word and language choices appropriate to the style and purpose of the text **Select from different presentational features** to suit particular writing purposes on paper & on screen	**Year 2** Use planning to establish clear sections for writing Use appropriate language to make sections hang together	**Year 2** Write simple and compound sentences and begin to use subordination in relation to time and reason **Compose sentences using tense consistently** (present & past) Use question marks, and use commas to separate items in a list	**Year 2** Write legibly, using upper and lower case letters appropriately within words, and observing correct spacing within and between words Form and use the four basic handwriting joins **Word process short narrative** and non-narrative texts

NC KS1 Programme of Study - Literacy

(revised framework objectives)

Numeracy 1 using and applying mathematics	Numeracy 2 counting & understanding number	Numeracy 3 knowing & using number facts	Numeracy 4 calculating	Numeracy 5 understanding shape	Numeracy 6 measuring	Numeracy 7 handling data
Year 1	**Year 1**	**Year 1**	**Year 1**	**Year 1**	**Year 1**	**Year 1**
Solve problems involving counting, adding, subtracting, doubling or halving in the context of numbers, measures or money, for example to 'pay' & 'give change' **Describe a puzzle or problem** using numbers, practical materials & diagrams; use these to solve the problem & set the solution in the original context **Answer a question** by selecting and using suitable equipment, and sorting information, shapes or objects; display results using tables and pictures **Describe simple patterns** and relationships involving numbers or shapes; decide whether examples satisfy given conditions **Describe ways of solving puzzles** and problems, explaining choices and decisions orally or using pictures	**Count reliably** at least 20 objects, recognising that when rearranged the number of objects stays the same; estimate a number of objects that can be checked by counting **Compare and order numbers,** using the related vocabulary; use the equals (=) sign **Read and write numerals from 0 to 20,** then beyond; use knowledge of place value to position these numbers on a number track and number line **Say the number that is 1 more or less than any given number,** & 10 more or less for multiples of 10 **Use the vocabulary of halves and quarters** in context	**Derive and recall all pairs of numbers with a total of 10** and addition facts for totals to at least 5; work out the corresponding subtraction facts **Count on or back in ones, twos, fives and tens** and use this knowledge to derive the multiples of 2, 5 and 10 to the tenth multiple **Recall the doubles of all numbers to at least 10**	**Relate addition to counting on;** recognise that addition can be done in any order; use practical and informal written methods to support the addition of a one-digit number or a multiple of 10 to a one-digit or two- digit number **Understand subtraction as 'take away'** and find a 'difference' by counting up; use practical and informal written methods to support the subtraction of a one-digit number from a one-digit or two-digit number and a multiple of 10 from a two- digit number **Use the vocabulary related to addition and subtraction and symbols** to describe and record addition and subtraction number sentences **Solve practical problems** that involve combining groups of 2, 5 or 10, or sharing into equal groups	**Visualise and name common 2-D shapes and 3-D solids** and describe their features; use them to make patterns, pictures & models **Identify objects that turn about a point** (e.g. scissors) or about a line (e.g. a door); recognise & make whole, half & quarter turns **Visualise & use everyday language to describe the position** of objects and direction and distance when moving them, for example when placing or moving objects on a game board	**Estimate, measure, weigh and compare objects,** choosing & using suitable uniform non-standard or standard units & measuring instruments (e.g. a lever balance, metre stick or measuring jug) **Use vocabulary related to time;** order days of the week & months; read the time to the hour & half hour	**Answer a question** by recording information in lists & tables; present outcomes using practical resources, pictures, block graphs or pictograms **Use diagrams to sort objects into groups** according to a given criterion; suggest a different criterion for grouping the same objects
Year 2	**Year 2**	**Year 2**	**Year 2**	**Year 2**	**Year 2**	**Year 2**
Solve problems involving addition, subtraction, multiplication or division in contexts of numbers, measures or pounds and pence **Identify and record the information or calculation needed to solve a puzzle or problem;** carry out the steps or calculations and check the solution in the context of the problem **Follow a line of enquiry;** answer questions by choosing and using suitable equipment and selecting, organising and presenting information in lists, tables and simple diagrams **Describe patterns and relationships** involving numbers or shapes, make predictions and test these with examples **Present solutions to puzzles and problems** in an organised way; explain decisions, methods and results in pictorial, spoken or written form, using mathematical language and number sentences	**Read and write two-digit and three-digit numbers in figures and words;** describe and extend number sequences and recognise odd and even numbers **Count up to 100 objects by grouping them and counting in tens, fives or twos;** explain what each digit in a two-digit number represents, including numbers where 0 is a place holder; partition two-digit numbers in different ways, including into multiples of 10 and 1 **Order two-digit numbers** and position them on a number line; use the greater than (>) and less than (<) signs **Estimate a number of objects;** round two-digit numbers to the nearest 10 **Find one half, one quarter and three quarters** of shapes and sets of objects	**Derive and recall all addition and subtraction facts for each number to at least 10,** all pairs with totals to 20 and all pairs of multiples of 10 with totals up to 100 **Understand that halving is the inverse of doubling** and derive and recall doubles of all numbers to 20, and the corresponding halves **Derive and recall multiplication facts for the 2, 5 and 10 times-tables** and the related division facts; recognise multiples of 2, 5 and 10 **Use knowledge of number facts and operations to estimate and check answers to calculations**	**Add or subtract mentally a one-digit number or a multiple of 10 to or from any two-digit number;** use practical and informal written methods to add and subtract two-digit numbers **Understand that subtraction is the inverse of addition and vice versa;** use this to derive and record related addition and subtraction number sentences **Represent repeated addition and arrays as multiplication,** and sharing and repeated subtraction (grouping) as division; use practical and informal written methods and related vocabulary to support multiplication and division, including calculations with remainders **Use the symbols +, -, ?, ÷ and = to record and interpret number sentences involving all four operations;** calculate the value of an unknown in a number sentence	**Visualise common 2-D shapes and 3-D solids;** identify shapes from pictures of them in different positions and orientations; sort, make and describe shapes, referring to their properties **Identify reflective symmetry in patterns and 2-D shapes** and draw lines of symmetry in shapes **Follow and give instructions involving position, direction and movement** **Recognise and use whole, half and quarter turns,** both clockwise and anticlockwise; know that a right angle represents a quarter turn	**Estimate, compare & measure lengths, weights and capacities,** choosing & using standard units (m, cm, kg, litre) & suitable measuring instruments **Read the numbered divisions on a scale,** and interpret the divisions between them (e.g. on a scale from 0 to 25 with intervals of 1 shown but only the divisions 0, 5, 10, 15 and 20 numbered); use a ruler to draw and measure lines to the nearest centimetre **Use units of time (seconds, minutes, hours, days) and know the relationships between them;** read the time to the quarter hour; identify time intervals, including those that cross the hour	**Answer a question** by collecting and recording data in lists and tables; represent the data as block graphs or pictograms to show results; use ICT to organise and present data **Use lists, tables and diagrams to sort objects;** explain choices using appropriate language, including 'not'

Programme of Study - Numeracy (revised framework objectives)

Sc1.1 planning	Sc1.2 ideas & evidence; collecting evidence	Sc1.3 comparing evidence	Sc2.1 life processes	Sc2.2 humans and other animals	Sc2.3 green plants	Sc2.4 variation and classification	Sc2.5 living things in their environment	Sc3.1 grouping materials	Sc3.2 changing materials	Sc4.1 electricity	Sc4.2 forces and motion	Sc4.3 light and sound
SC1 scientific enquiry			**SC2 life processes & living things**					**SC3 materials and their properties**		**SC4 physical processes**		
1.1a ask questions 'How?', 'Why?', 'What if'?) and decide how they might find answers to them	1.2a follow simple instructions to control the risks to themselves and to others	1.3a make simple comparisons (eg, hand span, shoe size) and identify simple patterns or associations, and try to explain it, drawing on their knowledge and understanding	2.1a differences between things that are living and things that have never been alive	2.2a recognise and compare the main external parts of the bodies of humans and other animals	2.3a recognise that plants need light and water to grow	2.4a recognise similarities and differences between themselves and others, and to treat others with sensitivity	2.5a find out about the different kinds of plants and animals in the local environment	3.1a use their senses to explore and recognise the similarities and differences between materials	3.2a find out how the shapes of objects made from some materials can be changes by some processes, including squashing, bending, twisting & stretching	4.1a about every-day appliances that use electricity	4.2a find out about, & describe the movement of, familiar things (e.g. cars going faster, slowing down, changing direction)	4.3a identify different light sources, including the Sun
1.1b use first-hand experience & simple information sources to answer questions	1.2b explore, using the senses of sight, hearing, smell, touch & taste as appropriate, & make & record observations & measurements	1.3b compare what happened with what they expected would happen, and try to explain it. Drawing on their knowledge and understanding	2.1b that animals, including humans, move, feed, grow, use their senses and reproduce	2.2b that humans and other animals need food and water to stay alive	2.3b to recognise and name the leaf, flowers, stem and root of flowering plants	2.4b group living things according to observable similarities and differences	2.5b identify similarities & differences between local environments & ways in which these affect animals & plants that are found there	3.1b sort objects into groups on the basis of their properties texture, float, hardness, transparency & whether they are magnetic or non-magnetic)	3.2b explore & describe the way some everyday materials) for example water, chocolate, bread, clay, change when they are heated or cooled	4.1b simple series circuits involving batteries, wires, bulbs and other components - eg buzzers	4.2b that both pushes and pulls are examples of forces	4.3b that darkness is the absence of light
1.1c think about what might happen before deciding what to do	1.2c communicate what happened in a variety of ways, including using ICT	1.3c review their work and explain what they did to others	2.1c relate life processes to animals and plants found in the local environment	2.2c that taking exercise and eating the right types and amounts of food help humans to keep healthy	2.3c that seeds grow into flowering plants		2.5c care for the environment	3.1c recognise and name common types of material & recognise that some of them are found naturally		4.1c how a switch can be used to break a circuit	4.2c to recognise that when things speed up, slow down or change direction, there is a cause	4.3c that there are many kinds of sound and sources of sound
1.1d Recognise when a test or comparison is unfair				2.2d about the role of drugs as medicines				3.1d find out about the uses of a variety of materials & how these are chosen for specific uses on the basis of their simple properties				4.3d that sounds travel away from sources, getting fainter as they do so, and that they are heard

2.2e how to treat animals with care and sensitivity

2.2f that humans and other animals can produce offspring and that these offspring grow into adults

2.2g about the senses that enable humans and other animals to be aware of the world around them

NC KS1 Programme of Study for Key Stage 1 - Science

NC KS1 Programme of Study - ICT

ICT 1 1.1 finding things out 1.2 developing ideas and making things happen		ICT 2 exchanging and sharing information	ICT 3 reviewing, modifying & evaluating work as it progresses	ICT 4 breadth of study
1.1a gather information from a variety of sources	1.2a use text, tables, images & sound to develop their ideas	2a share their ideas by presenting information in a variety of forms	3a review what they have done to help them develop their ideas	4a work with a range of information to investigate the ways it can be presented
1.1b enter & store information in a variety of forms	1.2b select from and add to information they have	2b present their completed work effectively	3b describe the effects of their actions	4b exploring a variety of ICT tools
1.1c retrieve information that has been stored	1.2c plan & give instructions to make things happen		3c talk about what they might change in future work	4c talk about the uses of ICT inside and outside school
	1.2d try things out & explore what happens in real & imaginary instructions			

NC KS1 Programme of Study - History

H1 chronological understanding	H2 K & U of events, people &changes	H3 historical interpretation	H4 historical enquiry	H5 organisation & communication	H6 breadth of study
1a place events and objects in chronological order	2a recognise why people did things, why events happened and what happened as a result	3a identify different ways in which the past is represented	4a find out about the past from a range of sources of information	5a select from their knowledge of history and communicate it in a variety of ways	6a changes in their own lives and the way of life of their family or others around them
1b use common words and phrases relating to the passing of time (for example, before, after, a long time ago, past	2b identify differences between ways of life at different times		4b ask and answer questions about the past		6b the way of life of people in the more distant past who lived in the local area or elsewhere in Britain
					6c the lives of significant men, women and children
					6d past events from the history of Britain and the wider world

NC KS1 Programme of Study - D&T

D&T 1 developing planning & communicating ideas	D&T 2 working with tools, equipment, materials	D&T 3 evaluating processes & products	D&T 4 k & u of materials & components	D&T 5 breadth of study
1a generate ideas	2a explore sensory qualities of materials	3a talk about their ideas	4a working characteristics of materials	5a focused practical tasks
1b develop ideas	2b measure, mark out, cut and shape	3b identify improvements	4b how mechanisms can be used	5b design & make assignments
1c talk about their ideas	2c assemble, join & combine materials			5c investigate & evaluate products
1d plan what to do next	2d use simple finishing techniques			
1e communicate ideas	2e follow safe procedures			

NC KS1 Programme of Study - Geography

G1.1 & G1.2 geographical and enquiry skills		G2 knowledge & understanding of places	G3 knowledge & understanding of patterns & processes	G4 knowledge & understanding of environment	G5 breadth of study
1.1a ask geographical questions	1.2a use geographical vocabulary	2a identify & describe what places are like	3a make observations about where things are located	4a recognise changes in the environment	5a the locality of the school
1.1b observe and record	1.2b use fieldwork skills	2b identify and describe what places are	3b recognise changes in physical & human features	4b recognise how the environment may be improved & sustained	5b a contrasting locality in the UK or overseas
1.1c express their own views about people, places & environments	1.2c use globes, maps & plans at a range of scales	2c recognise how places become they way they are & how they are changing			5c study at a local scale
1.1d communicate in different ways	1.2d use secondary sources of information	2d recognise how places compare with other places			5d carry out fieldwork investigations outside the classroom
		2e recognise how places are linked to other places in the world			

Programme of Study for Key Stage 1 - Art & Design

A&D1 exploring & developing ideas	A&D2 investigating & making art, craft and design	A&D3 evaluating & developing work	A&D4 k & u of materials & components	A&D5 breadth of study
1a record from first hand observation, experience & imagination	2a investigate the possibilities of materials and processes	3a review what they and others have done	4a visual and tactile elements	5a exploring a range of starting points
1b ask and answer questions about the starting points for their work	2b try out tools & techniques & apply these	3b identify what they might change	4b materials & processes used in making art, craft & design	5b working on their own, and collaborating with others
	2c represent observations, ideas and feelings		4c differences & similarities in the work of artists, craftspeople & designers	5c using a range of materials and processes
				5d investigating different kinds of art, craft & design

Programme of Study for Key Stage 1 - Music

M1 performing skills	M2 composing skills	M3 responding & reviewing (appraising skills)	M4 responding & reviewing (listening skills)	M5 breadth of study
1a use their voices expressively by singing songs, chants, rhymes	2a create musical patterns	3a explore and express their ideas and feelings about music	4a listen with concentration & internalise & recall sounds	5a a range of musical activities
1b play tuned & untuned instruments	2b explore, choose & organise sounds & musical ideas	3b make improvements to their own work	4b how combined musical elements can be organised	5b responding to a range of starting points
1c rehearse and perform with others			4c how sounds can be made in different ways	5c working on their own, in groups & as a class
				5d a range of live and recorded music

Programme of Study for Key Stage 1 - PE

PE1 acquiring and developing skills	PE2 selecting and applying skills, tactics and compositional ideas	PE3 evaluating and improving performance	PE4 knowledge and understanding of fitness and health	PE5 breadth of study
1a explore basic skills, actions and ideas with increasing understanding	2a explore how to choose & apply skills and actions in sequence & in combination	3a describe what they have done	4a how important it is to be active	5a dance
1b remember & repeat simple skills & actions with increasing control	2b vary the way they perform skills by using simple tactics and movement phrases	3b observe, describe & copy what others have done	4b recognise & describe how their bodies feel during different activities	5b games
	2c apply rules and conventions for different activities	3c use what they have learnt to improve the quality and control of their work		5c gymnastics

Programme of Study for Key Stage 1 - PSHE

PSHEC1 developing confidence & responsibility & making the most of their abilities	PSHEC2 preparing to play an active role as citizens	PSHEC3 developing a healthier lifestyle	PSHEC4 developing good relationships & respecting differences
1a recognise their likes & dislikes, what is fair & unfair, what is right & wrong	2a take part in discussions with one other person and the whole class	3a make simple choices that improve their health & wellbeing	4a recognise how their behaviour affects other people
1b share their opinions on things that matter to them and their views	2b take part in a simple debate about topical issues	3b maintain personal hygiene	4b listen to other people and play and work co-operatively
1c recognise, name and deal with their feelings in a positive way	2c recognise choices they make, & the difference between right & wrong	3c how some diseases spread and can be controlled	4c identify and respect differences and similarities between people
1d think about themselves, learn from their experiences & recognise what they are good at	2d realise that people and other living things have needs, & that they have responsibilities to meet them	3d about the process of growing from young to old & how people's needs change	4d that family and friends should care for each other
1e how to set simple goals	2e that they belong to various groups & communities, such as a family	3e the names of the main parts of the body	4e that there are different types of teasing & bullying, that bullying is wrong
	2f what improves & harms their local, natural & built environments	3f that household products & medicines, can be harmful	
	2g contribute to the life of the class and school	3g rules for, and ways of, keeping safe, basic road safety	
	2h realise that money comes from different sources		

Credits and references

The following organisations and individuals have kindly given permission for photographs to be used in this book:

ASCO Educational

Web sites included in this book (in alphabetical order):

www.42explore.com/smplmac - links to lots of websites for simple mechanics

www.4to40.com - has instructions for a mini-dustbin drum

www.360models.co.uk - an architectural model site - look at their gallery of models for ideas

www.artistshelpingchildren.org - has a page on making your own musical instruments

www.athropolis.com/links/how-work - how lots of things work

www.ascoeducational.co.uk - educational supplier

automata.co.uk/pulleys - for moving figures

www.bbc.co.uk - the BBC has a Gardening with Children section

www.bbc.co.uk/parenting/play_and_do/primary_outdoor - outdoor games for 7-11 year olds

www.bbc.co.uk/tyne/weather - for weather station instructions

www.bbc.co.uk/weather/weatherwise/activities - for useful information for adults and children

www.bbsrc.ac.uk/society/schools/primary/minibeast/discovery2.pdf - a leaflet on Making Bug boxes

www.bingbangbong.info - make outdoor musical instruments and sound makers

www.brio.co.uk - will give you stockists for their child-size gardening tools

www.buildingcentre.co.uk - is the centre for the building industry

www.butlersheetmetal.com - make your own steel drum

www.cabe.org.uk - Commission for Architecture and the Built Environment (CABE)

www.cheerleading.org.uk/schools - where you can download a free leaflet on starting cheerleading in your school!

www.cheshire.gov.uk/ecoschools/Eco_Games - is a site that encourages children to invent their own games with sticks and other natural objects, or play the ones on the site.

www.communityplaythings.co.uk the best, most long-lasting wooden bricks are from Community Playthings

www.cookson-mcnally.co.uk/playspaces - supply performance areas for schools, you could look here for ideas

www.diydoctor.org.uk/projects/laybricksandblocks - has a sheet on block building with real bricks

www.dorsetforyou.com/media/pdf/r/b/Pre_school_outdoor_environment.pdf - for a downloadable booklet on outdoor play with a section on tyres

www.ecocentric.co.uk - sell a model castle and other toys made from recycled cardboard

www.education-show.com - has information about outdoor music suppliers

www.eduzone.co.uk - education supplier

www.ehow.com/how_1276_build-block-tackle - make a block and tackle

www.ehow.com/how_1277_make-simple-pulley - make a pulley

www.ehsni.gov.uk - environmental heritage site with booklets to download

www.ers.north-ayrshire.gov.uk/minibeasts - minibeast information

www.find-me-a-gift.co.uk - has a great photo of a giant Ludo set you could use as an idea

www.fi.edu/weather - for making a weather station

www.freenotes.net - an American firm that installs outdoor musical equipment - good picture gallery

www.freegames.eu.comwww.gameskidsplay.net - games compendium site

www.funandgames.org - and click through to games for hundreds of different games to play

fun.familyeducation.com/Children's-science-activities/weather - and find the activity 'rain in a bag'

www.greatgardengames.com - a site that sells big size garden games - good for ideas www.insectlore.co.uk - have butterfly kits and lots of other insect resources and information about keeping and investigating insects

www.kidsonthenet.org.uk - is a creative writing site for children

www.kidscape.org.uk - has a leaflet on safer, nicer playtimes

www.leics.gov.uk/foundation_maths_outside.doc - a download of ideas for the Foundation Stage, but still useful for KS1

www.literacytrust.org.uk - or for information on story sacks

www.llanddulas.conwy.sch.uk - where you can find some good videos of how to play some of the best playground games

www.ltl.org.uk - the Learning Through Landscapes website

www.linepainting.net - more ideas for playground markings

www.make-stuff.com/kids - has some great projects including a cardboard castle

www.mikids.com/Smachines - for pulleys

www.mindstretchers - supply a range of innovative materials for exploration out of doors

www.mudcat.org/kids/drums - for simple home-made drums

www.naturegrid.org.uk - QCA ideas on growing things

www.newitts.com - for playground chalk, cones and markers for games

www.nncc.org - has more information on rhythm

www.novelties-direct.co.uk - has a great selection of cheerleader pompoms at reasonable prices

www.ntseducation.org.uk - investigation pack

www.nwt.org.uk - for a Minibeasts.pdf - leaflet

www.oakthorpe.enfield.sch.uk/tour - is a school with an outdoor stage

outreach.rice.edu - teacher materials

www.pioneer.cwc.net/playgroundpals.htm - takes you to a whole list of sites with ideas for playground games

www.playgroundfun.org.uk - is a site for children, with a range of different games and tips for adults on using them in school

www.playquest.co.uk - make playground markings and have some good ideas in the photos on their website, as well as giant chess and draught pieces

www.rhs.org.uk - Royal Horticultural Society and click on 'plant finder'

www.saps.plantsci.cam.ac.uk - download leaflet on growing seeds

www.sciencetech.technomuses.ca/english/schoolzone/activities - pulley activity sheet

www.scienceyear.com/under11s/playground - download a free leaflet with ideas for painting your own playground games

www.spacekraft.co.uk - for ribbon sticks, 'body sox' lycra suits, latex tube band for group work

www.sport-thieme.co.uk - to see examples of cheerleader equipment

www.standards.dfes.gov.uk/pdf/primaryschemes - has the QCA scheme of work for a unit of work for Years 1/2 on 'feel the Pulse - Exploring Pulse and Rhythm'

www.standards.dfes.gov.uk/schemes2/science - DfES guidance on growing things www.standards.dfes.gov.uk/parentalinvolvement/pics/pics_storysacks - for information on story sacks

www.storysack.com - Neil Griffiths' site for his ready made story sacks for the primary age range

www.sunclocks.com - for some pictures of paintings on a playground

www.sustainweb.org - growing plants by planting seeds such as fruit pips and stones

www.sutton.gov.uk - for a minibeast workpack

www.teachingideas.co.uk/music - gives some ideas for simple rhythm activities

www.terragenesis.co.uk - model castle using textured paint

www.thekidsgarden.co.uk - recycling for kids

www.tts-group.co.uk - education suppliers who have a range of tools and barrows etc

web.ukonline.co.uk/conker/pond-dip/tadpoles - for information about keeping tadpoles

www.worcestershire.gov.uk - where you can download a free leaflet on outdoor music

www.ypte.org.uk/docs/factsheets/env_facts/minibeasts - Young People's Trust for the Environment - good information and activities

www.woodlands-junior.kent.sch.uk - a school site with playground games including a giant version of Connect

www.worcestershire.gov.uk/home/09_play_mark.pdf - download a free leaflet on making playground markings

en.wikipedia.org/wiki/Playground_games - playground games

NB
These websites and addresses are correct at the time of printing. Please let us know if you find other interesting sources or contacts sally@featherstone.uk.com.

Carrying on in Key Stage One

Other titles in this series include:

Construction

Sand

Water

Role Play

and

Sculpting, Stuffing and Squeezing

www.acblack.com/featherstone

The EYFS – Birth to Three

Little Baby Books offer lots of ideas for working with young children, and match the original birth to three framework.

A Strong Child **A Skilful Communicator** **A Competent Learner** **A Healthy Child**

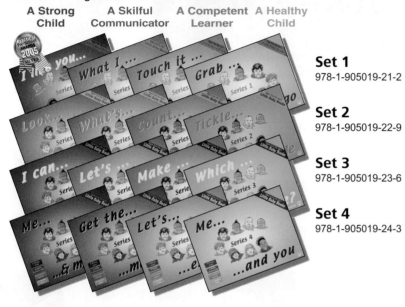

Set 1
978-1-905019-21-2

Set 2
978-1-905019-22-9

Set 3
978-1-905019-23-6

Set 4
978-1-905019-24-3

Also available with the activities grouped according to stage.

Book 1 Heads-up Lookers & Communicators (124pp)
978-1-905019-50-2
Book 2 Sitters, Standers & Explorers (156pp)
978-1-905019-51-9
Book 3 Movers, Shakers & Players (172pp)
978-1-905019-52-6
Book 4 Walkers, Talkers & Pretenders (238pp)
978-1-905019-53-3

All the activities in these books are suitable for the EYFS. Just look for the component and age you need.

Heads-up Lookers & Communicators — Stage 1: 0-8 months

Sitters, Standers & Explorers — Stage 2: 8-18 months

Movers, Shakers & Players — Stage 3: 18-24 months

Walkers, Talkers & Pretenders — Stage 4: 24-36 months

Foundations Activity Packs

Ages 3–5

Each pack: ● pbk, resources & CD £24.99 ● 305 x 225 mm
● 48pp ● colour photographs, black and white illustrations

These award-winning activity packs are bursting with resources – ideal for all adults working with children aged 3–5.

Written by Early Years practitioners and experts.

"Everything you need to plan, organise and lead activities on early years themes"
Montessori International

The resources in each pack include:
● **50+ easy-to-follow activities**
● **14 photocopiable activity sheets**
● **8 colour photocards**
● **CD of poems, songs and stories**
● **Giant themed display poster**
● **Planning chart**

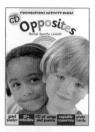

Celebrations
Kate Tucker
9780713668452

Opposites
Rachel Sparks Linfield
9780713662191

My School Day
Ann Montague-Smith
9780713661583

Minibeasts
Christine Moorcroft
9780713662184

Playsongs

Livelytime Playsongs
Sheena Roberts & Rachel Fuller
Early Years practitioner/ parent resource:
● **£9.99**
● **pbk (32pp) + CD**
9780713669404

Baby's active day in songs and pictures.
A picture songbook which tells the story of a baby's day in glorious full colour and in songs with clearly described actions. Dances, peekaboo, finger and toeplays, teasers, knee bouncers and lullabies. 0–3 years

Sleepytime Playsongs
Sheena Roberts & Rachel Fuller
Early Years practitioner/ parent resource:
● **£9.99**
● **pbk (32pp) + CD**
9780713669411

Baby's restful day in songs and pictures.
A picture songbook and CD which tells the story of baby's restful day in glorious full colour and in songs with clearly described actions. 0–3 years

Playsongs
Early Years/practitioner/ parent resource:
● **£12.99**
● **pbk (48pp) + CD**
9780713663716

72 songs and rhymes for babies and toddlers.
The perfect musical start for the very young – fully illustrated book and CD. 0–3 years

Continuity and progression through the EYFS

The Baby & Beyond series takes simple activities or resources and shows how they can be used with children at each of the EYFS development stages, from birth to 60+ months. Each double page spread covers one activity, so you can see the progression at a glance.

Shows how simple resources can be used by children at different ages and stages

Ideal to support progression and extend learning.

Inspiration for planning continuous provision

To see our full range of books visit www.acblack.com